Penguin Books

The Beginner's Guide to Satellite TV

Richard Maybury has been deeply interested in all aspects of electronics since his schooldays and went on to study electronic engineering prior to joining Thorn EMI in the early 1970s. He spent four years there working on colour television, remote control and teletext systems. His career in journalism followed on from his freelance activities with the electronic industry magazine *Electronics Today International*.

His first full-time job in publishing was as Editorial Assistant on *Computing Today*. Soon after he became Assistant Editor of *Hobby Electronics* and simultaneously Technical Editor of the newly launched *Video Today* and *Which Video?* During this period Richard Maybury became involved in the video industry and wrote a book on video and a book on computers, and collaborated on several more. Following a series of features on space technology and a visit to the Kennedy Space Center in Florida, he was invited to attend the launch of the first Space Shuttle in April 1981.

In 1981 he became editor of *Citizen's Band* and in 1982 he collaborated with Terry Bentley to create and launch the science and technology magazine *Next* ... In 1984 they teamed up again to form the editorial services company in TEXT ..., which originates and produces magazines including *Which Video? and Satellite TV* (of which Richard Maybury is the editor) and articles for various book and magazine publishers.

Richard Maybury

The Beginner's Guide to Satellite TV

PENGUIN BOOKS

Penguin Books Ltd, Harmondsworth, Middlesex, England
Viking Penguin Inc., 40 West 23rd Street, New York, New York 10010, U.S.A.
Penguin Books Australia Ltd, Ringwood, Victoria, Australia
Penguin Books Canada Ltd, 2801 John Street, Markham, Ontario, Canada L3R 1B4
Penguin Books (N.Z.) Ltd, 182–190 Wairau Road, Auckland 10, New Zealand

Published in Penguin Books 1987

Copyright © Richard Maybury, 1987
All rights reserved

Made and printed in Great Britain by
Richard Clay Ltd, Bungay, Suffolk
Filmset in 10 on 13pt Sabon

Except in the United States of America, this book is sold subject
to the condition that it shall not, by way of trade or otherwise, be lent,
re-sold, hired out, or otherwise circulated without the
publisher's prior consent in any form of binding or cover other than
that in which it is published and without a similar condition
including this condition being imposed on the subsequent purchaser

Contents

Introduction 7
Chapter 1: What is satellite TV? 11
Chapter 2: From cable to satellite 20
Chapter 3: Hardware in the home 25
Chapter 4: Programming 47
Chapter 5: Space hardware 58
Chapter 6: Implications 65
Appendices
　Appendix 1: Domestic satellite systems for under £1,500 70
　Appendix 2: Technical data and addresses 91
　Appendix 3: Programme providers and management organizations 104
Glossary 112

Introduction

At this moment over twenty television channels are being beamed directly at every home in western Europe from orbiting satellites 36,000 kilometres above the equator. Most of us are completely unaware of these transmissions and, until very recently, reception was impossible on anything less than highly sophisticated and prohibitively expensive electronic equipment.

That was yesterday. Today those signals can be picked up on equipment that is available in almost every high street for less than £1,000. In less than five years there could be as many as one hundred television channels to choose from, and the equipment will cost less than £200 at today's prices. Stick around – we are at the very beginning of a revolution in communications and broadcasting that is potentially every bit as important as Marconi's first tentative clicks and buzzes!

The concept of transmitting television signals from orbiting satellites is far from new: the basic idea behind today's communications network was first proposed over forty years ago by science-fiction writer Arthur C. Clarke in an article written in 1945 for *Wireless World* magazine. His calculations showed that an orbiting satellite, situated 36,000 kilometres above the Earth and travelling at 11,000 kilometres per hour in the same direction as the planet's own rotation, would appear to remain stationary in the sky from any given point on the ground. The so-called 'geostationary' principle is at the heart of all contemporary intercontinental telecommunications. Dozens, perhaps hundreds, of geostationary satellites now encircle the Earth, relaying speech, computer data, television pictures and military intelligence from one point to another.

Ever since the invention of the telegraph, man has striven to communicate over ever greater distances, but before the advent of radio the sender and receiver always had to be connected together physically by wire. Radio opened up immense possibilities for truly long-distance communications, but until relatively recently it was not possible to accommodate the immense number of two-way speech channels required for a national or international telephone network into a conventional radio link. This would have entailed sacrificing huge areas of the limited radio spectrum otherwise allocated to the various forms of broadcasting. Local, national and international telephone networks have, therefore, been linked together by multi-way cables containing many thousands of individual wires. The cost of, say, linking the UK directly to Australia by wire is both technically and economically prohibitive.

It wasn't until the US and Russian space programmes got under way in the early 1960s that the first communications satellites were put into orbit. Early satellites did little more than passively reflect signals, transmitted from earth stations, as they passed overhead. Later, as both the orbiting technology and launch systems improved, satellite payloads increased sufficiently to enable active repeater transmitters to be put into orbit; these were used to relay signals over huge distances and, by using newly developed electronic encoding techniques and ultra-high-frequency radio bands, managed to squeeze many hundreds of voice channels into relatively small portions of the radio spectrum. In addition to voice channels, some early communications satellites also had extra experimental capacity for vision signals.

The first live transatlantic television pictures relayed by satellite were broadcast in 1962, using the celebrated Telstar. Telstar's activities were cut short in 1963, after an active life of only four months, by electromagnetic radiation caused by an American high-altitude nuclear bomb test. Telstar 2 was launched three months later and continued to operate for two years. Operation of these early satellites was severely limited by their low-altitude orbits, which restricted the amount of time they remained in range of ground-based tracking stations. The advantages of geostationary operation were well understood by this time, but it took three abortive attempts, using the Syncom series of satellites, before Syncom 3 was established in a 36,000-kilometre orbit, in time to relay the 1964 Olympics from Japan to the US.

In 1964 the International Telecommunications Satellite Organization, better known as INTELSAT, was formed by a group of nations including Great Britain and the US. Today, with over one hundred member nations, INTELSAT owns, launches, controls and regulates all of the huge network of commercial, industrial and scientific communications satellites, among which are a number designed specifically to relay television signals.

The orbiting television relay platforms were primarily intended as a low-cost linking and distribution system for national networks and cable TV operators. Signals sent up to the satellites from the TV companies are retransmitted back to Earth and picked up by specialized receiving equipment within each satellite's reception area, or 'footprint'. This technique is now the basis for an entirely new form of broadcasting, whereby TV signals are beamed directly to the viewer's own receiver instead of being redistributed via cable networks or local ground-based transmitters.

Currently hundreds, sometimes thousands, of ground-based transmitters are needed to cover the uneven terrain of even a relatively small and flat country such as Britain. Within the last few years the cost of placing a geostationary satellite in orbit has fallen sufficiently to rival the expense of installing, maintaining and operating terrestrial transmitting equipment. Today, even with the phenomenally high costs and risks involved with space technology, it is, or soon will be, economically advantageous for many countries to put a high-power television satellite into orbit.

Direct broadcasting by satellite (DBS) technology relies upon geostationary transmitters some twenty to thirty times more powerful than those currently in use. This, in turn, will mean smaller receiving antennae. Whereas the present generation of dishes has to be at least 1.2 metres in diameter, DBS antennae should be small enough to fit unobtrusively on to the roof or side of any building. Mass production of domestic receiving equipment will, it is to be hoped, lead to a smaller outlay for the consumer, and more channels mean a greater choice – that is the positive side of TV from space.

There is a dark side, however, which we shall look at in greater detail later on in this book. Among the most important attributes of satellite television transmitters are their virtual immunity to deliberate jamming and their almost total disregard of geopolitical boundaries, unlike their ground-based counterparts. The possibilities for propagandizing and manipulation of information by the programme originators are almost endless, whether they are trying to sell one brand of washing powder across six European countries or political ideals to the population next door.

For good or ill, satellite TV will almost certainly become one of the most pervasive and persuasive information and entertainment media on or, more correctly, above this planet. Satellite TV is here, right now, but it is new technology and we have only just begun to learn how to manage and exploit its huge potential. It is possible that, when future historians look back at the last few years of the twentieth century, we may be seen as participants in one of the most important experiments in the history of global communications – let us hope that it has a happy ending!

Chapter 1: What is satellite TV?

In effect, satellite television is no different from any other form of TV, apart from the path followed by the radio frequency signal from the transmitting aerial to the receiving aerial. The programme material can be as interesting, varied, dull or predictable as any other form of broadcasting, but the opportunities and possibilities opened up by this revolutionary form of broadcasting go far beyond the present limitations of conventional terrestrial television.

Land-based TV transmitters throughout Europe and the rest of the world broadcast radio frequency signals in the VHF (very-high-frequency) and UHF (ultra-high-frequency) bands. Unlike medium-wave (MW) or long-wave (LW) transmissions, these high-frequency signals are readily absorbed or, at best, drastically weakened by solid objects.

TV signals tend to travel in straight lines and remain largely unaffected by reflective layers in the Earth's atmosphere; lower frequencies are bounced back to Earth by reflective layers in the upper atmosphere, permitting radio reception over hundreds, sometimes thousands, of miles. VHF and UHF signals can normally be picked up only when the receiving aerial is aimed directly at the transmitter mast, which is generally sited on high ground to maximize the area of coverage.

Essentially, satellite television is no different to this method,

The Beginner's Guide to Satellite TV

except that the transmitter aerial is located on an orbiting spacecraft 'parked' in a geostationary orbit 36,000 kilometres above the equator. Clearly it would be impractical to build a complete television station in space, so the programme material is transmitted up to the satellite from a ground station, and the satellite beams the signal back to Earth. Highly directional antennae aboard the satellite carefully direct the signal in a predetermined pattern known as the 'footprint'.

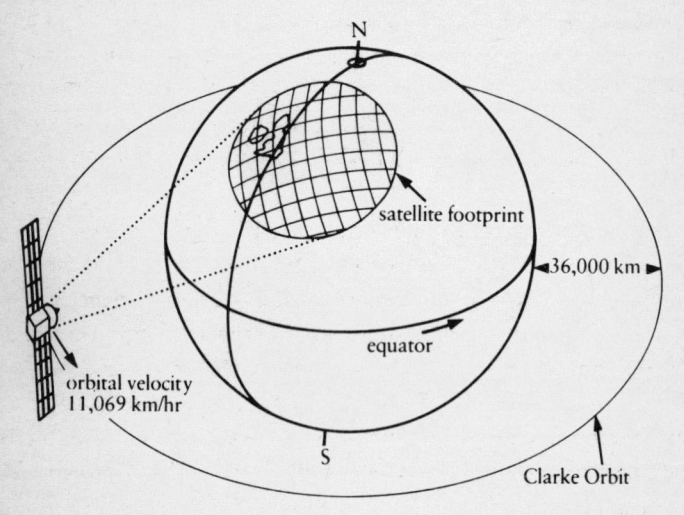

Figure 1: Principles of geostationary orbit and satellite footprint

Thus, anyone within the satellite's footprint, equipped with suitable receiving apparatus, will be able to watch these programmes; but why should anyone bother to go to such lengths when terrestrial television offers local, national and international coverage based on far more accessible technology?

The answer is, or at least soon will be, one of economics. Satellites already offer cheaper and more effective methods of signal distribution – in spite of the costs and risks involved in designing, building and launching spacecraft. One satellite could theoretically broadcast television programmes to an entire continent; three such satellites could cover the whole world. Compare that with the current situation, in which hundreds, sometimes thousands, of land-based transmitters are used to cover even a relatively small country such as Britain.

The origins of today's satellite television began in the early 1970s, hard on the heels of a worldwide boom in telecommunications. Much of the credit must go to the US for launching a highly successful network of communications satellites, designed primarily to carry two-way speech and data circuits within an international telecommunications system.

Excess or spare capacity on some satellites was leased to major television networks on a relatively informal basis. Originally they used satellites to provide links between distant studios, to pass programme material between stations. It proved to be a highly economical alternative to existing land-line and microwave links and rapidly developed into a more substantial relay system, used to distribute network programme material across the continent. Programmes from centralized TV studios in New York and Los Angeles could be moved cheaply and effectively to land-based transmitters or cable TV stations serving small, sometimes isolated local communities in areas where land links would be prohibitively expensive.

Cable-system operators were among the first to really exploit satellite links by offering their subscribers additional channels relayed from other towns and cities across the country.

The sky's the limit

Entirely new channels rapidly emerged, using the expanding satellite distribution network to carry their material into millions of homes. This type of distribution allowed these newly established television stations to operate at far lower costs than the national networks, yet the combined effects of cable and satellite links enabled them to reach the same kind of national audience at a fraction of the cost of maintaining a land-based transmission system.

On paper, at least, satellite TV (STV) appears to be a very attractive proposition. However, it is unwise to assume that terrestrial television will ever disappear altogether, at least not in the foreseeable future. Although the expense of maintaining land-based transmitters is undoubtedly high, the technology is easily repairable and replaceable. If a TV satellite fails, for whatever reason, it could take months, possibly years, to replace. A land-based transmitter can normally be repaired in a matter of hours.

More importantly, terrestrial transmitters offer an unrivalled degree of flexibility. Geostationary satellites, based on present and known future technologies, cannot carry more than a small number of television channels. Even with dozens of satellites it would be impossible to offer the kind of localized community services that are characteristic of the UK and many European national TV networks.

Most of today's communications satellites, now used to relay television signals, were not originally designed just for broadcasting television programmes. Their primary role was, and still is, for telecommunications purposes; television pictures are carried on a strictly commercial basis, using spare capacity that is leased to television companies by satellite operators and owners. The power levels generated by the spacecraft transmitters are relatively low by comparison with terrestrial standards, so receiving dishes and equipment have to be particularly sensitive in order to receive these extremely weak signals.

A wholly new generation of satellites is due to go into service over the next ten years. These satellites are specifically designed to broadcast directly to individual homes, the signals being picked up on small, compact rooftop antennae and inexpensive receiver units; the first of these DBS satellites are due to be in operation by 1987. Although these new satellites will operate at high power levels, much of the equipment currently in use will still operate satisfac-

What is satellite TV?

torily, though it is possible that some modifications to the equipment will have to be made. In either case, whether the signals come from high-, low- or even intermediate-power satellites, the path followed by the transmissions is exactly the same.

The first part of the television picture's journey begins with the 'programme provider'. This will normally be a company set up specifically to produce television programming for cable and satellite distribution. Material from the programme provider is sent to a local 'earth station', either directly, via land-line or microwave links, or in a prerecorded form on videotape or film. At the earth station the programme material is converted into a form suitable for transmission to the satellite. The signals are then fed to a large parabolic dish antenna that beams them, in the form of microwave radio signals, up to the geostationary satellite. This part of the transmission path is known as the 'uplink'.

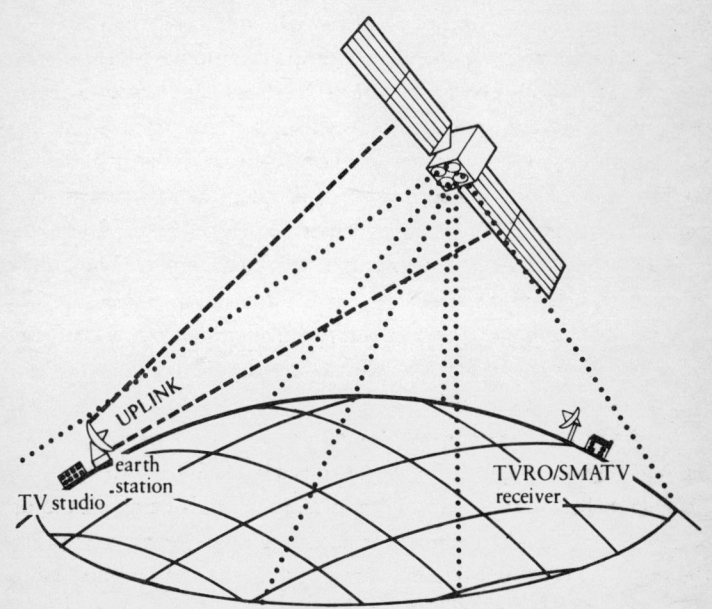

Figure 2: Transmission path of STV signals

The earth station can be situated almost anywhere with a clear, unobstructed 'view' of the spacecraft. One satellite can be served by dozens of earth stations, spread over an entire continent if necessary.

Once aboard the satellite, the incoming signals are simultaneously retransmitted back to Earth in predetermined patterns, or footprints. Each satellite may be equipped with several 'steerable' antennae, which allow a high degree of flexibility. This whole process is known as 'transponding'; thus, a single satellite may have as many as twenty transponders, each capable of relaying one or more television channels or several thousand speech or telephone channels. The majority of satellites in use at the moment carry only a limited amount of television material; most will be devoted to carrying telephone and data transmissions as part of an intercontinental telecommunications network.

Cable changes

Until the 1980s the television signals carried by satellites were generally picked up on large parabolic dish antennae (known as 'master' antennae), from which they were fed, via cable, to paying subscribers. At that time STV receiving equipment would have been far beyond the resources of most private individuals, who, in any case, would have needed to find space for massive receiving dishes.

This method of signal distribution is better known as SMATV (satellite master antenna television); it is a simple, cost-effective way of moving television signals over large distances and was, until the advent of domestic satellite television, potentially very profitable for the cable companies and programme providers. Funding is very straightforward: each household connected to a cable network pays the cable company a monthly or yearly subscription for receiving the programmes. The cable company pays the programme

What is satellite TV?

providers for supplying the material and the programme providers pay the satellite owners and operators for use of a transponder.

The situation would have remained simple and straightforward were it not for a series of largely unexpected advances in electronics technology. It was a spin-off from the microchip industry that changed the situation, one of those remarkable developments that continue to make so many important and dramatic changes in all our lives.

Prior to the mid 1970s satellite transmissions could be received only on large parabolic dish antennae up to 4 metres in diameter; these had to be coupled to expensive and unwieldy receiving apparatus. Today satellite signals can be picked up thoughout much of Europe on dishes as small as 1.2 metres in diameter. When the first generation of DBS satellites comes into service, the size of receiving antennae will fall to less than 1 metre and the cost of receiving equipment could soon be less than one-third of today's prices.

Although much of the technology employed in all present satellite television is vastly different to normal TV broadcasting, most of the differences are unseen by the viewer, who requires only a specialized antenna or dish and a small, unobtrusive 'black box' to connect to his existing TV set.

Conventional land-based television signals are broadcast at frequencies of between 400 and 800 megahertz (1 megahertz = 1,000,000 cycles per second) on the UHF band throughout most of Europe; most satellites in use over Europe use transmission frequencies of between 10 and 12 gigahertz (1 gigahertz = 1,000,000,000 cycles per second), some twenty times higher in frequency than a normal TV signal – a frequency band close to the limits of affordable, mass-produced technology. Limits are continually being pushed further forward, however, and the costs associated with satellite technology have fallen to a point where it can legitimately be described as a domestic product.

In truth, all this has happened rather faster than most experts would have predicted. DBS satellites have been an industry goal for many years. In the late 1970s it was anticipated that DBS satellites would be operational by the 1990s at the earliest, at which time the cost of domestic receiving equipment would be a viable proposition for most households. The forecasters were correct in their assumption but failed to foresee the situation that confronts us today: low-cost domestic equipment capable of picking up STV signals from the present generation of low-power telecommunications satellites. Such 'domestic' systems have been available in North America since the early 1980s and, to a lesser extent, in Europe since 1984. Now, following UK Government deregulation, STV equipment is freely available in the UK and many EEC countries.

Not surprisingly, this situation has created an unforeseen intermediate stage in satellite broadcasting in which signals primarily intended for redistribution to cable networks are available, apparently free of charge, to anyone possessing the appropriate equipment. Naturally this has not gone unnoticed and various attempts are now being made to prevent unauthorized reception by 'scrambling' or encrypting the signal (see pp. 50–51) in order to obtain subscriptions directly from owners of STV equipment, who will need to hire or lease unscrambling devices.

Single domestic satellite receiving stations, or TVROs (television receive-only installations), are now at the centre of a battle that will become even more confused as new satellites are launched towards the middle of 1987. Medium-power satellites, a kind of halfway-house between current low-power communications satellites and DBS systems, will carry a number of channels intended to reach the TVRO market on small- to medium-sized dishes (1.0 to 1.5 metres in diameter). More importantly, however, some channels will be 'advertising-driven'. Revenue will be obtained from advertisers, who will doubtless appreciate the opportunity to parade their wares in front of millions of potential customers across the whole of Europe. Scrambling or encrypting signals could be seen as limiting, as viewers would naturally be reluctant to pay twice for the privilege of watching STV material: once in unscrambling equipment and a second time in the hidden costs that manufacturers add on to their products to pay for advertising. If the cost of a television-licence fee charged in most European countries is also taken into account, there is a chance that satellite television could price itself out of business.

On the positive side, the international coverage offered by satellite television has the potential to attract audiences many times the size of those that could be reached with land-based transmitters. Language need not be a barrier: each vision signal can be accompanied by several sound channels, one for each of the countries within the satellite's footprint. Simple electronic switching circuits within a satellite receiver can automatically select the appropriate sound signal. Additional audio channels can also be used for high-quality stereo sound or separate radio channels; a number of existing programme providers already exploit this feature.

The future of satellite technology holds a number of intriguing possibilities, including high-definition vision signals that would be equivalent in quality to the kind of reproduction previously possible only in a cinema. Satellite television is in its infancy and much of what is to come can only be guessed at. However, one thing is clear: the next ten years will see an accelerating pace of development in all forms of communications that could make the last one hundred years appear as if we were standing still . . .

Chapter 2: From cable to satellite

Broadcasting television programmes from orbiting satellites is clearly a most attractive option for those who control, produce and distribute television programmes. Using established technology, three satellites could comfortably broadcast to the whole world, replacing hundreds of thousands of terrestrial transmitters. But how did it all begin?

The current situation arose more by accident than design; technology has advanced far faster than anyone could have predicted, and the price, size and complexity of STV equipment have fallen dramatically in the past ten years. However, until the advent of DBS, satellite television signals currently receivable in the UK and much of Europe were, and still are, primarily intended for redistribution by cable TV network operators.

Despite ambitious cabling plans proposed by the UK Government in the early 1980s, Britain remains largely reliant upon a network of land-based television transmitters. This is in spite of the numerous well-documented advantages to both the consumer and the cable operator. At the very least revenue collected from subscribers can be used to fund additional programme material directly, over and above nationally networked channels that are normally carried on cable networks as a matter of course.

Cable television has a number of important qualities. It relies upon a direct-wired connection between the viewer's television and the cable distributor. Thus it is possible to establish a two-way audio or electronic link between the viewer and the cable station. This opens up a number of interesting possibilities, including the now familiar spectacle of live-audience participation in certain types of light entertainment shows (usually talent shows, when viewers can voice their opinions by voting for particular acts).

A second, more important option exists whereby the viewer's television set can be connected to distant computers using systems now widely known as teleshopping and telebanking. Products and services can be ordered and paid for using a simple microprocessor-controlled digital keypad connected to the cable-linked receiver. The services on offer are displayed on the viewer's screen; he then responds by pressing the appropriate buttons. Payment is made directly by giving details of the viewer's credit card or bank account number.

Unfortunately many of the existing cable systems in Britain were installed during the 1950s, mainly in fringe reception areas. The signal-carrying capacity of the early cables was often restricted to half a dozen vision and one or two sound channels, barely enough to carry the four prime channels. High-capacity cable systems have been installed in the past twenty years, usually in new urban developments where the disruption caused by cable-laying is not a problem. In addition, older systems are being updated, but it is unlikely that cable TV in Britain will ever reach the same levels as those in the US or on the Continent.

Why should that be? The reasons are threefold. Firstly, the actual process of physically connecting a home by cable to a TV studio is considerably more difficult in Britain. The obvious method of using underground telephone conduits has been vigorously opposed by the Post Office (now British Telecom), which has argued that there isn't any room left in its conduits for additional cabling, and that only trained BT engineers can be trusted to maintain such a vital service – inexperienced cable operators could damage the telephone system. This type of attitude has not been a problem in the US and much of Europe, where most household electrical services such as power and telephone lines are distributed above ground on cables suspended between poles. Cable TV tends to come in 'piggy-backed' on these services.

Secondly, in geographical terms the UK is relatively small, so establishing a national and regional network of television transmitters has been less difficult, technically and economically, than it would have been in, say, the US and the more mountainous regions of Europe.

Thirdly, Britain is in the almost unique position of having four high-quality TV channels, supplied by the BBC and IBA. Their popularity is confirmed by the high proportion of British households owning video cassette recorders. Market research shows that they are used primarily for 'time shifting': recording off-air programmes that are to be watched at a more convenient time. Moreover, time shifting often occurs while the television is switched on and tuned to another channel. In addition, the UK has one of the most highly developed video film rental markets in the world. A typical specialist rental shop will carry some 2,000 titles (with access to some 20,000 films), all of which are available for a modest overnight hire charge. Such is the popularity of UK programming that several cable TV networks in Europe actually carry BBC 1 and 2!

Will the same factors affect the popularity of satellite television in Britain? On the face of it, STV offers a similar kind of multi-channel service but without the additional benefits of a directly linked cable system. It is possible, of course, but highly unlikely.

Alternative programming

Programme material intended for transmission by cable networks reaches the cable station, or 'head end', by a variety of different means. Most cable networks carry a selection of alternative

From cable to satellite

channels over and above the 'must-carry' material (normally one or more national or state-operated TV stations). These additional channels generally include local community channels, programming aimed at ethnic minority groups and more general entertainment programming such as first-run films, pop videos, soap operas, news and sports.

Locally produced material usually originates in the cable operators' own in-house studios, or is produced by community groups using their own technical resources. Some cable material is distributed in a prepackaged form on video tape that is delivered to the cable station by courier or parcel service. Another alternative is land-line or microwave relay, although for reasons of cost and technical complexity this tends to be less common in larger countries where networks may be widely dispersed or situated in mountainous areas.

The most recently developed method involves the use of geostationary satellites to relay programme material over hundreds, even thousands, of miles. The technology used in satellite communications has been established for over twenty years and, despite well-publicized problems with launch vehicles, the contemporary communications satellite is now the most efficient, reliable and cost-effective way of moving television pictures around the globe.

The tremendous growth of the domestic satellite television market is due largely to a small group of American electronics enthusiasts who discovered that it was possible to pick up signals from the satellites using mainly home-built equipment. Home STV pioneers in the late 1970s were able to pick up dozens of pay-to-view channels, available, apparently, for free. However, commercial interests rapidly moved in, and by the early 1980s satellite TV receiving systems were readily obtainable over the counter. Programme providers have been involved in a running battle with TVRO owners and have tried various methods to prevent unauthorized reception of their signals. At the time of writing this problem has yet to be fully resolved.

A similar situation has existed in Europe for the past five years, but with one important difference: the transmission frequencies used by the majority of US satellites are much lower than those used in Europe, typically 3 to 4 gigahertz compared with European systems operating on or around 10 to 12 gigahertz. Until very recently this would have precluded any kind of DIY market, as both the technology and design tolerances of receiving equipment would have been beyond the resources of even the most adventurous electronics enthusiast. However, it is now possible to put together a complete system from scratch using off-the-shelf electronic modules. It is even possible to construct a dish antenna from readily obtainable materials.

Chapter 3: Hardware in the home

The equipment needed to receive satellite television pictures relies on advanced electronic principles, though most of the equipment now available in the UK is as simple to operate as the average video recorder or washing machine!

A basic STV system has three main components: the receiving antenna plus its mount and stand; the microwave head, or LNB (low-noise block converter); and the tuner, or demodulator. Don't worry too much about the jargon; technospeak is rife in satellite television and tends to disguise the fact that domestic STV systems are basically 'black boxes' that require absolutely no technical expertise to operate.

The dish antenna

Geostationary satellites retransmitting TV signals beamed up from earth stations are situated some 36,000 kilometres (26,000 miles) above the Earth's equator. Satellites rely upon electrical power derived from large solar panels deployed after launch, backed up by rechargeable batteries. However, even the most efficient solar panels cannot generate more than a tiny fraction of the power used by terrestrial TV transmitters. The combination of distance, absorptive effects of the atmosphere and limited power largely dictate the satellites' transmitting frequencies. However, other considerations have to be borne in mind; these include interference to and from terrestrial radio sources, as well as such things as radar and the general background noises of natural and man-made electromagnetic radiation.

For these reasons most satellites receivable over Europe use the 'KU-band, which covers frequencies in the region of 10 to 12 gigahertz (10,000,000,000 cycles per second); needless to say, such signals can only be picked up by sensitive and sophisticated electronic equipment. As these transmissions are so weak, it is necessary to capture as much of the signal as possible using a specialized antenna: the type most frequently used is the now familiar parabolic reflector dish.

KU-band signals share many of the characteristics of visible light, so dish-type antennae are similar in construction to concave mirrors, focusing the incoming signal to a single point where the microwave head, or LNB, is situated. Clearly the larger the dish the greater the signal captured (though an STV system's efficacy is also dependent upon a number of other factors including the efficiency of the LNB – more about that on pp. 34–6).

The parabolic shape chosen by many dish manufacturers is just one possible option, however, and a number of other configurations are becoming increasingly popular. There are two main ways of beaming the signal on to the LNB: directly (with the LNB mounted at the dish's prime focus) or indirectly, with a second reflector placed at the focal point, which then 'bounces' the signal to the LNB (which is mounted in a more convenient position).

The main problem with a simple direct-feed parabolic dish is the tripodlike structure, or 'milkstool', supporting the LNB. It tends to cast a 'shadow' on to the dish, cutting out a sizeable proportion of the incoming signal. One alternative is to mount the LNB on a single mounting pole fixed to the centre of the dish. This is known as a 'buttonhook' feed, due to the hooklike bends in the mounting

Hardware in the home

direct-feed (prime focus) parabolic

indirect-feed (cassegrain) parabolic

direct-feed (offset) parabolic

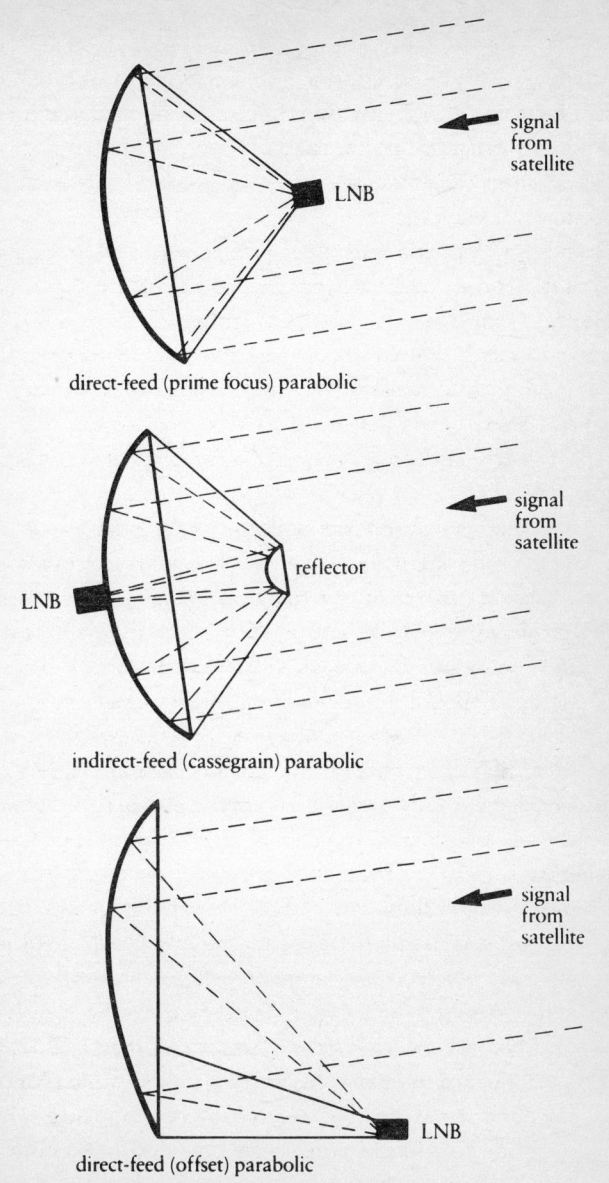

Figure 3: Types of dish antennae and feeds

pole which ensure that the LNB is sited at the dish's focal point. The shadow can be eliminated altogether by using an 'offset' parabola, where the focal point of the dish is outside the path of the incoming signal. Offset dishes are normally elliptical in shape, although at least one manufaturer now produces a square dish. Offset dishes can be expensive, but they are generally more efficient than similarly proportioned parabolic antennae.

Indirectly fed dishes are more commonly used for transmitting, or on larger receiving antennae to lessen the weight burden of the microwave head. However, at least one domestic 1.5 metre indirect-feed type dish uses the 'cassegrain' configuration, whereby the LNB is mounted in the centre of the dish with a conical sub-reflector sited at the focal point. The second type of indirect-feed dish is the 'Newtonian feed', which is similar to the cassegrain but with a tubular waveguide that is mounted on the LNB and pointing at an inverted conical reflector mounted at the focal point. This type of set-up is almost exclusive to larger dishes.

Apart from the various shapes and sizes of dishes now available on the domestic market, a variety of different materials and techniques are used in their construction. Dishes as small as 1.2 metres in diameter can be used in the UK to receive KU-band signals from low-power satellites, although accuracy of curvature and construction must be to a very high standard, even on dishes up to 2 metres in diameter.

The most common method of manufacturing simple parabolic shapes under 2 metres in diameter is to press or spin the dish from one thin sheet of aluminium and to mount it on to a rigid metal frame in order to preserve its shape. Both spinning and pressing are relatively quick and cheap, but the equipment required is very expensive and bulky, and will only repay the manufacturers' capital outlay with large production runs. Small numbers of one-off metal dishes can be economically produced using an explosive-forming technique. Here a thin sheet of metal is placed over a hollow former in a tank of water. An explosive charge is detonated over the sheet and the explosion presses the sheet into the former in a fraction of a second.

Although aluminium is both cheap and light, thin-gauge dishes above 1.5 metres in diameter often need expensive reinforcement to prevent them deforming under their own weight or in heavy winds. Dishes made from sheet steel would be rigid enough to be self-supporting, but the weight penalty is a problem. In order to get around this, some manufacturers have developed dishes made from perforated steel, which weigh marginally more than one-piece aluminium designs but do not require any additional reinforcement.

Dishes above 2 metres in diameter are normally made in several sections in order to maintain a rigid structure. This is known as 'petalized' construction, due to the symmetrical petal-like shapes that are bolted together to form the dish.

In the past five years an increasing number of manufacturers have developed dishes made from a variety of plastic materials, including fibreglass, or GRP (glass-reinforced plastic). The main advantage of fibreglass dishes is that they are ideally suited to short production runs or one-offs and can be economically tailored for specialized applications. Unfortunately, the trade-off is the relatively slow construction process, which involves building up layers of fibreglass matting and resin. Plastic dishes, on the other hand, can be produced by conventional injection-moulding techniques, but normally the maximum size is limited to under 1.5 metres due to the cost and complexity of the moulds. For this reason most plastic dishes are of the elliptical offset type that is generally more rigid and more efficient than similarly sized parabolic shapes.

The primary advantage of plastic and fibreglass dishes is their built-in rigidity, which negates the need for any additional reinforcement. Normally, strengthening ribs are moulded on to the back of the dish, along with the lugs for the mounting bracket. There are drawbacks, however: in order for the dishes to reflect effectively the weak signals, the plastic or resin has to be impregnated with metallic particles or, in the case of some GRP dishes, a layer of metal foil.

Several designs for home-built dishes have appeared in American books and magazines for intrepid DIY enthusiasts. In general, however, these are practicable only for antennae above 3 metres in diameter, for which manufacturing tolerances can be wider. In truth these are really suitable only for the lower frequency 'C' band transmissions used by many US satellites. None of these, unfortunately, is generally receivable in Europe on domestic STV systems. At least one UK manufacturer is marketing a DIY dish kit: although the constructor must design and build the stand and mount, the fibreglass dish is supplied ready-built and requires only finishing and weatherproofing.

Receiving dishes are exposed to the weather twenty-four hours each day, so effective weatherproofing is essential. This is especially true for aluminium dishes, which are prone to corrosion from acid rain. Most manufacturers treat their dishes with a protective plastic film, paint or anodized finish. Plastic and GRP dishes generally do not need any additional treatment, although some types of plastic can deform and degrade in strong sunlight, and fibreglass can develop a kind of rot if the protective outer layer is not thick enough or re-treated frequently enough.

The mount

Precision is the keynote in any satellite installation, whether it is a large commercial installation or a 1.5 metre domestic set-up. In both cases the receiving antenna has to be aimed at a point in space some 36,000 kilometres above the equator with an accuracy that has to be within a fraction of a degree. There are now hundreds of satellites circling the Earth in the so-called 'Clarke Belt' (named after Arthur C. Clarke), so it is imperative that

Hardware in the home

both the satellite and the receiving dish are very accurately aligned.

Although the satellite is in a fixed geostationary orbit, the effects of the Earth's gravity and solar winds do tend to pull the spacecraft away from its allotted position (a nominal 'box' 70 miles square that is agreed by international consent). Small thruster rockets and centrifugally operated orientation equipment, under control from ground stations, can normally be relied upon to maintain the satellite in its place – after all, it would be rather difficult, not to say expensive, to send up a manned rocket to do it manually.

Back on the ground, the same level of precision is necessary to keep the dish antenna pointing in exactly the right direction in the face of strong winds, rain, snow, hail, perching birds and careless knocks. This highly demanding task is handled by the mount and stand – a strong rigid structure that has to withstand the effects of every conceivable natural element, and quite a few unnatural ones too . . .

There are basically four types of mount used in domestic STV installations: fixed, elaz, polar and motorized. Taking them in order, a *fixed* mount is simply that: a simple rigid metal fitting designed to hold the dish in one position. Fixed mounts are normally little more than metal brackets, designed to attach the dish to a metal pole or similar fixture. Construction is usually very simple and cheap, not to say basic, but they are designed to be fixed and forgotten. The main disadvantage is that realignment on to another satellite can be both difficult and time-consuming.

The *elaz* (sometimes 'azel') mount takes its name from the two most basic alignment parameters used in setting up a satellite dish: elevation and azimuth. Elevation is the angle of tilt, measured in degrees in relation to the horizon. Thus, a satellite directly overhead would have an elevation of 90 degrees (in practice all geostationary satellites are directly over the equator, which means that from the UK they appear low in the southern sky – typically 20 to 30 degrees above the horizon). A satellite's azimuth angle, or bearing, is measured with respect to magnetic north. Satellites in the Clarke Belt describe an arc crossing the southern sky; the two main satellites beaming TV signals at the UK are located around 16 degrees east and 30 degrees west of due south.

An elaz mount, therefore, has two planes of movement: it allows the dish to rotate on an axis and to tilt up and down. Therefore once the elevation and azimuth angles of a particular satellite are known, the dish can be aligned precisely, using relatively simple instruments such as a compass and an inclinometer. Elaz mounts are normally fairly simple in construction and once a satellite has been located they are 'locked-off' by tightening two or more bolts. Realignment to another satellite can be as simple or as complicated as the construction of the mount and stand allows.

The *polar* mount is basically an extension of an elaz mount, except that once adjusted it has only one plane of movement that allows the dish to track accurately the arc described by the Clarke Belt. This is usually accomplished by mounting the dish on a swivelling bracket that is inclined to the Earth's horizontal plane. Polar mounts have to be very accurately aligned, but once set up the single movement allows fast and precise realignment to any receivable satellite. In addition the single plane of movement means that it is a relatively straightforward proposition to fit a *motor* drive – which is the fourth and final type of mount we'll be looking at.

Motor mounts are normally based on polar mounts and incorporate a long extending arm that moves the dish from side to side. They have to be accurately controlled, usually by remote systems housed in or alongside the receiver equipment. Motorized actuators are normally mains-powered and require additional cabling from the indoor unit to the dish.

The stand is the final component in the antenna structure; its job is self-explanatory and, as a simple rule of thumb, the bigger the better. In an ideal domestic installation the stand should be rigidly bolted to a concrete base, to ensure accuracy of alignment and to

Hardware in the home

prevent the dish from blowing over in strong winds. A dish provides a formidable wind break and can be subject to tremendous stresses even in quite light winds. Generally speaking, the UK rarely experiences hurricane force winds (above 75 mph), although gusts of over 100 mph have been measured in some areas of Scotland. For this reason most dishes and stands have a wind-loading factor, or a measurement of their ability to withstand strong gusts, and some manufacturers even quote a 'destruction' loading, which is the point at which the structure can be expected to fail. Stands and dishes with wind loadings of 70 mph and above are normally adequate for the UK, although a reputable dealer will normally advise of any special precautions that need to be taken for a given location.

There is no such thing as a typical antenna installation, and the actual costs of erecting and aligning a dish can vary from as little as £50 to well over £300. Depending upon the complexity of the installation, it can take from a couple of hours to several days – this is rarely spelt out in advertising and promotional literature!

A dish must be mounted in a position that gives a clear line of sight to the satellite; this normally entails mounting the dish and its stand in a back garden, although the side of a building or suitable roof structure can also be used. A dish antenna has to be rigidly mounted so that it can be aimed precisely at the satellite to within a fraction of a degree. However, because there are at least two satellites of interest to UK viewers (transmitting on two different polarities), the mount and microwave head will need to be realigned (either manually or using motorized actuators) in order to receive all twenty channels.

The dish and its stand are the key components in any installation. Quite simply, no two sites will ever be alike. On ground-level installations a flat, concrete platform is clearly the best solution. The stand can be directly bolted to the concrete base, either with expanding 'Rawlbolt' type fittings or with 'chemical' bolts (which encase themselves in a hardening resin when a seal is broken).

A second option with some kinds of stand is to dig a pit a foot or two deep, which is then half filled with hardcore. The stand is placed in the hole and concrete poured over it. This kind of set-up can be returfed (if it is in the middle of a lawn, for instance) to make it appear less instrusive.

A less permanent but equally secure arrangement is to 'stake' the mount to the ground using metal fence-post sockets that are hammered into the ground to a depth of two feet. These are then used as anchors for a metal or wooden frame to which the stand can be bolted. A more permanent solution is to bolt the stand to heavy precast concrete slabs or kerbstones, which can be obtained from local DIY stores for a few pounds.

Mounting an antenna on to the side of a building or a flat roof calls for special care, as the dish will usually be in a more exposed position and subject to strain from high winds. Flying dishes can be expensive, not to say dangerous, and at least one death in the US has been attributed directly to falling satellite antennae.

Microwave head

The microwave head is normally mounted on a tripod-like structure, or 'milkstool', at the focal point of a receiving dish, though there are a number of variations, depending on the dish's construction. Wherever the head is mounted, however, it has one primary task to perform, and that is to collect and amplify the extremely weak signals coming in from the dish (without adding to the high levels of electromagnetic noise also picked up by the dish). In this instance the head is normally referred to as a low-noise amplifier (LNA).

Microwave heads used on domestic TVRO dishes in Europe normally include additional circuitry to convert the signals to a lower, more manageable frequency. These are generally called low-noise converters or low-noise block converters (LNC or LNB).

Down-converting incoming signals of 10 to 12 gigahertz to around 1 gigahertz in an LNB is an important technique, one that allows the signal being fed to the set-top receiver/demodulator to be carried in relatively low-cost coaxial cable over several tens of metres without the need for additional amplification. Cables capable of carrying KU-band signals would be prohibitively expensive and, in addition, the signals would be subject to heavy losses, requiring amplification every few metres.

This apparently straightforward task relies, in fact, upon electronic components working at or near the limits of the semiconductor industry's ingenuity, and in many TVRO packages the LNB is the single most expensive component in the whole receiving system. Indeed, it is the development of the low-cost LNB that has made reasonably priced TVRO systems a commercial reality. The key component inside the head is a device known as a gallium arsenide field effect transistor (GasFet for short), which was originally developed in Japan during the early 1970s. Prior to that the only devices capable of operating at such high frequencies were known as parametric amplifiers: highly complex circuits that were capable of operating only at extremely low temperatures. This usually meant that they had to be cooled by immersion in liquid nitrogen.

The types of LNB used in most domestic TVRO installations require a power supply of 18 to 20 volts DC. Although it is perfectly feasible to run a supply line to the LNB alongside the main signal-carrying cable, most manufacturers use the coaxial cable to carry the DC supply as well. The presence of DC and signal voltages on the same cable is not a problem, and the DC supply can be used to power other equipment also in the system, such as amplifier modules (for cable runs over 100 metres) and motorized polarity actuators or polarators.

This brings us to polarization and polarators. In order to maximize the capacity of a satellite transponder, electronic engineers designing satellite transmission systems utilize a technique known as polarization. This allows two signals of similar frequencies to be transmitted from a single transponder without one interacting or interfering with the other. Currently two polarization systems are in use, the most common being horizontal and vertical polarization. This is rather similar in principle to the polarization of light – the effect can be observed with 'polarized' sunglasses. Each lens is constructed to allow only light of a single polarity to pass through. As white light is made up of light of many different polarities, only a limited amount of the light will pass through the lens. By holding one lens in front of the other, it is possible to stop almost all of the light from passing through by slowly rotating them in relation to each other. Radio frequency signals can be made to behave in a similar manner, so that signals of opposite polarity will not affect each other, even though they are coming from a single source.

A number of transponders aboard newly launched satellites will be broadcasting circular polarization transmissions; here signals are given a corkscrewlike twist in either a clockwise or anticlockwise direction.

An LNB is generally designed to pick up signals in one plane only, so in order to receive signals transmitted on the alternate plane it has to be manually (or mechanically, using a motorized actuator) rotated through 90 degrees.

A polarator is a small motorized device that automatically rotates the LNB as a whole or a small waveguide inside the feedhorn. Alternatively, some types of polarator have a series of metallic vanes that 'twist' the signal through the required angle.

Gain and noise

Natural and man-made electrical noise occurs randomly within every molecular structure, and is a constant problem with all forms of electronic circuitry. But in satellite receiving systems (parts of which deal with extremely weak high-frequency transmissions) electrical noise is an important design consideration and one of the most significant factors when determining a system's overall performance.

The LNB bears the brunt of the responsibility in the receiving chain when measuring the influence of noise on the signal as a whole, and its noise-related characteristics should be one of the main criteria when deciding upon a system. The various forms of noise present in TVRO systems are generally expressed as a logarithmic ratio known as a decibel, or just dB. Put simply, engineers measure noise in a signal before and after it has been through a particular stage of the system. As far as LNBs are concerned, the theoretical ideal is 0 dB, although this can never be achieved in practice. Recent advances in LNB design have yielded noise figures below 2 dB, and this is a good benchmark to bear in mind when comparing manufacturers' specifications. Some manufacturers quote noise figures for the system as a whole; a good average to aim for would be in the region of 10 dB or less.

Noise in an LNB is directly related to the temperature of its surroundings and, more importantly, the ambient temperature of the signal source – that is, a point in space 36,000 kilometres above the equator. Space is very cold, around $-270\,°C$; thus LNBs are said to have a 'noise temperature' figure. Ideally this should be as close to the temperature of space as possible, i.e. $-270\,°C$ to $-200\,°C$ is a good average. In practice noise temperature is quoted in degrees Kelvin, which can be simply converted from degrees Celsius by adding 273.

Feedhorn

One of the most important components in a dish antenna system is the feedhorn, a simple-looking tubular arrangement attached to the front of the LNB. In fact, the feedhorn has a critical job to do and one that will greatly affect the quality and strength of the received signal. On most domestic TVRO systems the most commonly used type is known as a 'scalar' feed: its job is to channel as much of the focused signal beam as possible from the dish into the LNB, while at the same time blocking out any extraneous radiation – a formidable task, considering the incredibly weak signal levels involved. Feedhorns that are used to receive horizontally and vertically polarized signals normally have a rectangular-shaped orifice: this serves to reduce crosstalk between signals of opposing polarity.

The feedhorn's other main function is to support the LNB in a precisely defined position in relation to the reflected signal beam from the dish. If the feedhorn is too close to the dish, it will not pick up all of the signal that is theoretically available. If it is too far from the focal point, the feedhorn will 'see' around the rim of the dish and pick up 'earth noise', which will also degrade the signal.

Scalar feedhorns are generally constructed from a lightweight alloy, and are either cast or machined directly from blocks of metal. Although a feedhorn is, in effect, little more than a tube, the end pointing towards the dish is faced with a flange composed of a series of concentric rings machined or cast into the metal; these are designed to increase the overall gain of the LNB by reflecting back on to the dish any portion of the signal that missed the feedhorn's opening. It also gives the component extra strength and permits a simpler design for the support structure.

Most types of feedhorn have a thin plastic cap, or membrane, made from electromagnetically 'transparent' material, over the open end of the feedhorn to weatherproof the LNB and protect it against the potentially damaging effects of insect invasion. LNBs normally bolt directly on to the back of the feedhorn. The open end is clamped into a support structure that allows the whole assembly to be rotated through 90 degrees for picking up vertically or horizontally polarized signals.

Hardware in the home

The tuner, or demodulator

Unlike dishes and LNBs there is a considerable diversity of designs among satellite tuners, ranging from simple black boxes with just a couple of knobs to complex computer-controlled terrors that wouldn't look out of place on the flight deck of Concorde.

The tuner, or demodulator, sometimes referred to as the 'indoors unit', is, in many respects, like an FM stereo radio tuner in a hi-fi component system. Its function is to detect, select and then process a single transmission from numerous other signals coming in from the aerial. This is then converted into a form usable by other pieces of equipment within the system – in the case of an STV tuner the aerial is a parabolic dish antenna and the equipment it is feeding will normally be a colour television receiver and/or a video recorder.

Although STV transmissions are on much higher frequencies than land-based TV broadcasts, the actual sound and vision signals are presently encoded in more or less the same way as terrestrial signals; in the case of the UK and much of Europe, this is the PAL or SECAM standard (Phase Alternate Line and Séquentielle Couleur à Mémoire; see Glossary). This means that once processed, STV transmissions can be viewed directly on almost any colour television receiver. There are two exceptions, however. Transmissions originating from France and the Soviet Union that use the SECAM system are one; these will appear in black and white on a UK TV receiver. Scrambled or encrypted transmissions, which we will look at in greater detail on pp. 50–51, are the second exception.

Signals from the tuner are fed into a TV receiver in exactly the same way as from a video recorder; that is, through the set's aerial socket. Transmissions are normally viewable on a spare station (tuned to channel 36), and STV channel selection is left up to the tuner. In recent years many TV receivers have been fitted with sockets for direct audio and video connections. These generally give improved picture and sound quality; most, if not all, currently available STV receivers have connections on their back panel for direct A/V connection. It is also worth pointing out that many satellite channels transmit teletext services similar to the British CEEFAX and ORACLE services; these too can be picked up using any suitably equipped TV receiver.

At least four different audio frequencies and transmission standards are used on European satellite channels. However, most STV tuners take these variations into account and are able to operate on all commonly used standards.

Built-in or set-top

There are two basic types of STV tuner available at the moment: those built into the cabinet of a TV receiver and set-top receivers, which plug into an existing colour television. Built-in STV tuners are presently of interest only to owners of a just a few upmarket brands of TV and make up only a tiny fraction of the systems available at the moment.

Connections

The connections between a typical STV tuner and a television receiver are almost exactly the same as those used with a video recorder. Nearly all satellite tuners have two sockets on the back panel marked 'RF' or 'UHF' input and output. The coaxial lead from the receiver's normal TV aerial is plugged into the STV tuner's RF (or UHF) input socket. A second lead (usually supplied by the manufacturer) connects between the STV tuner's RF (or UHF) output socket and the television receiver's aerial socket. To receive satellite signals the TV set must be tuned to the STV tuner's output. This is normally assigned to one of the TV's spare channels. TV sets already connected to a VCR should have the STV tuner connected between the VCR's RF input socket and the aerial. In this case it might be necessary to retune the VCR or STV tuner's RF output to avoid co-channel interference.

Hardware in the home

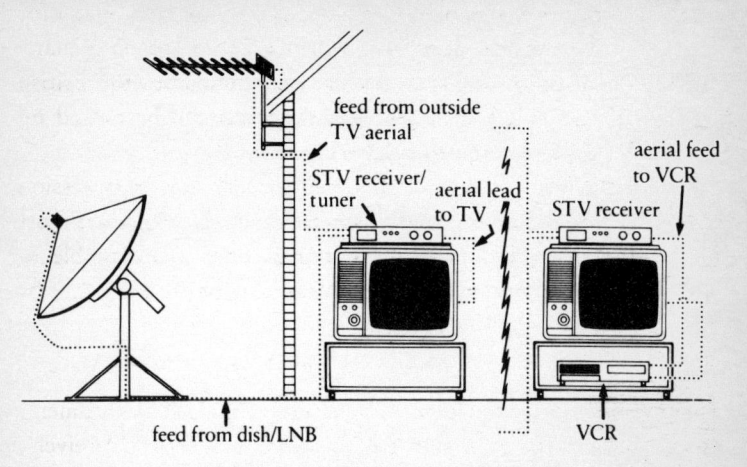

Figure 4: Connections to a TV set/VCR

One or two of the cheaper (or older) STV tuners do not have aerial or RF bypass circuits, so it is necessary to unplug the TV aerial socket and replace it with the STV tuner's RF output lead. Picture quality can be improved by using the STV receiver's and the TV's A/V sockets (where fitted); the dealer or installer will usually be able to supply the correct leads.

Operation

Set-top STV tuners generally have one of three different types of tuning system. The simplest (and cheapest) is the manually operated, continuously variable knob-type tuner. It works in exactly the same way as a rotary tuner on a simple radio receiver. Most STV tuners with rotary controls have some kind of scale or dial to help locate channels. Operation is almost foolproof, although the obvious drawback is that the viewer will have to get up out of his seat and twiddle the controls manually. Tuners of this type cannot be equipped with remote controls.

The second most common type of tuner uses pre-set, or push-button, tuning. These are similar in principle to the tuners fitted to most TVs and VCRs. They normally have between eight and ten tuner buttons, each of which is pre-set using a bank of thumbwheels or miniature tuner knobs hidden away behind a flap or door somewhere on the tuner.

Push-button tuners are simple to operate, reliable and, again, almost foolproof. The main drawback is the limited number of pre-sets that can be fitted, mainly due to the space restrictions imposed by the bulky mechanical push-buttons and their pre-set controls. However, this is not necessarily an insurmountable problem. At the moment there are rarely more than eight channels available at any given time, and, in any case, it is a simple matter to retune a spare pre-set to cater for little-used channels. Such limited capacity may become a problem in the near future when there could be as many as thirty or forty channels, however.

The third and most recent type of tuner uses a technique known as voltage synthesizer, or sweep, tuning. The technique originated on television receivers and has recently become a standard feature on many types of video recorder, replacing the older push-button type tuners, which in turn replaced rotary-dial tuners. Sweep tuners have almost unlimited capacity (though in practice they are usually limited to a manageable number). An STV tuner fitted with this type of channel selection can normally be programmed to tune, or 'scan', through the band until it 'locks' on to a transmission. The setting is then consigned to an electronic memory that the viewer can call up at any time. Such a system is eminently suitable for remote-control operation. Not surprisingly, the main drawback is complexity, which is normally reflected in the price. In all other respects, however, this type of tuner is preferred, as it is usually easier to operate, less prone to failure and able to cope with changing demands.

Hardware in the home

Controls

Satellite TV tuners often have additional controls and connectors that are rarely, if ever, found on other consumer electronic equipment. Here are some of the more common examples.

The rotary *audio tuning* control that is fitted to some tuners operates in the same way as the tuning control on a radio receiver. It enables the tuner to select the appropriate audio channel for a particular transmission. Some STV channels have three or four audio channels (some are used for alternative-language soundtracks for right and left stereo channels).

The *bandwidth* control is used to open up the tuner's signal processing circuitry in order to capture weak or erratic signals. The trade-off is normally reduced picture quality or increased interference ('sparklies').

AFC, or *automatic frequency control switches*, lock the tuner's signal detector circuitry on to a particular transmission, reducing the chance of signal drift. In some circumstances, such as during periods of low signal strength (heavy rainstorms, etc.), it may be necessary to unlock the AFC and retune the receiver.

Buttons or switches marked *polarity*, *x* or *y* or *horizontal/vertical* are used to control motorized polarators mounted on the LNB, to change from one polarity to the other. Sockets on the tuner's back panel, normally marked *polarity control*, connect between the tuner and the polarator.

Controls marked *audio select* or *J17* are used to resolve the different types or standards of audio signals used by some STV channels – this is not to be confused with the audio tuning control discussed previously. The majority of channels now use a common system of audio transmission, although on receivers the audio channels may sound distorted. This control will normally clear up the sound.

One of the potentially most important connections that should be fitted to every STV tuner is usually marked *baseband* or *unclamped* video. The output from this socket is designed to be fed into a decoder unit that may one day be necessary in order to view deliberately scrambled or encoded pay-to-view channels.

Signal strength meters, or displays, are used to give a relative indication of the strength of the incoming signals. Such displays can be particularly useful when aligning or repositioning an antenna.

RF level sockets are intended as an aid to installation engineers. A suitable test meter connected to this socket gives a readout of the signal strength coming into the receiver, which can be used to help with dish alignment.

An increasing number of new tuner designs are being fitted with *antenna positioning circuitry*. These control the dish actuator motor, which is fitted to a polar-type mount. Operation is usually via a pair of buttons marked 'east' and 'west'. Depressing either of the buttons moves the antenna, and a two- or three-digit display on the tuner's front panel gives a relative indication of position. Some more advanced designs have provision for 'direct entry'. By entering a two- or three-digit code into the receiver, the dish will automatically move to its new position. A further enhancement, as yet available only on very expensive equipment, ties the dish position in with tuning and polarity information, so, for instance, pressing a single channel button will automatically align the dish, tune the receiver and select the appropriate polarity. This feature is likely to become more common as production costs continue to fall.

Displays and indicators

There's little or no need for flashing and winking lights on STV equipment (leave them to the budget hi-fi systems). The only information the viewer really needs is the channel number or tuning position, the LNB polarity (where appropriate) and, at a pinch, signal strength. The latter can be no more than a simple LED (light-emitting diode) lamp that glows when the tuner is on a channel (similar to a stereo indicator on an FM radio). Meters and bar graphs are useful during the alignment, but tend to be little more than a distraction in normal use. There are exceptions, however, on installations that are regularly realigned from one satellite to another. In this case a signal strength meter is a useful tuning aid.

Add-ons and accessories

Most STV systems are designed, from the outset, to be upgradable. This approach allows the dealer to sell a basic package at a low-enough price to attract volume sales. If convenience features were sold with the basic system, its cost would certainly be prohibitive – but, as the bug bites, consumers will no doubt want to add these to their systems. The two most popular add-ons at the moment are polarators and actuators. However, an increasing number of 'basic' systems now include polarators as standard, and this trend is likely to continue. Motorized actuators designed to track the dish across the Clarke Belt can work only on stands fitted with polar mounts; it therefore makes sense to opt for this type of stand from the outset. The motorized actuator normally comes with an antenna positioner unit; this will usually sit alongside the tuner. The positioner's job is to control the actuator's movements and give an indication of its position, usually via a two- or three-digit LED display. Some more advanced types have built-in memories that will automatically align the dish to one or more pre-set positions.

Although the European domestic satellite TV market is still some way behind that of the US, the accessory market is developing rapidly. One of the most popular items is a dish alarm. Theft of LNBs and even dishes themselves is likely to become an increasingly troublesome problem. A simple 'trembler' type alarm, fitted to the stand to detect any movement, is one of the simplest options. At least one STV tuner has a built-in alarm. It works by monitoring the electrical connection between the receiver and the LNB. If the connection is tampered with for any reason, the alarm will sound.

Most LNBs will happily operate over a wide range of temperatures, although certain components inside these devices work best when they are warm; indeed, an LNB often takes a few seconds to 'warm up' in cold weather. For this reason many tuner designs keep the LNB permanently 'live', even though the tuner itself may be off or in the 'standby' mode. Not surprisingly, LNB 'cosies' have been developed to keep them warm during exceptionally cold spells. However, this is unlikely to be a problem in the UK, as temperatures rarely drop low enough to be a real problem.

To the enlightened, a satellite dish is a thing of great beauty; there are, however, a few sorry souls who regard them as intrusive eyesores. To alleviate their concern, a number of artistic individuals are now offering to paint dishes, either to blend in with their surroundings or, for those untroubled by philistine neighbours, in almost any colour scheme you can imagine . . .

Chapter 4: Programming

Generally speaking, the twenty or so satellite channels presently receivable in the UK and most of western Europe fall into two broad categories: general entertainment and special interest. Foreign-language channels make up a possible third category, although these can usually be classified under one of the two main headings, particularly if viewers are language students or if they speak a popular language.

Distribution of television programmes via cable and satellite systems highlights one major difference between these new media and traditional broadcast television. Normal television channels occupy large chunks of the radio spectrum, which is a finite resource. The VHF and UHF bands set aside for television broadcasting under international agreements could, in theory support several hundred channels, although in practice VHF and UHF signals have low penetrative properties, unlike short-wave signals, which are reflected over hundreds, sometimes thousands, of miles by the Earth's ionospheric layers. Even the most powerful TV transmitters have a relatively short range, normally no more than twenty to thirty miles. In order to overcome these problems, broadcasters have to install large numbers of transmitters to give full national coverage. Transmitter frequencies in adjacent areas and countries must be carefully chosen in order to avoid interference with each other. Thus, the usable channels in any given location are limited to a relatively small number – rarely more than ten to fifteen.

Cable and satellite systems, however, are unfettered by such constraints. A typical single-wire cable system can carry over thirty channels, and systems based on fibre-optic technology could carry twice that number. The theoretical capacity of an international satellite broadcasting network is quite staggering. An STV antenna tracking the Clarke Belt can pick out over twenty satellites – that comes to around 400 possible channels! Clearly it would be impossible and indeed impractical to handle that much material, but, based on the present situation, even a basic STV system can now pick up around twenty channels from four satellites.

Parallel programming

The potentially enormous capacity offered by cable and satellite systems encourages programme companies to provide highly specialized material targeted at specific groups of people, a technique known as 'parallel programming'. Parallel programming has a number of interesting advantages for the viewer, programme provider and advertiser. In a typical multi-channel cable or satellite system, the viewer has a wide selection of material from which to choose: up to thirty channels is not unusual on some US and Continental cable networks. Single-subject channels will be of direct and specific interest to a particular group of viewers throughout the day. Conventional general entertainment programming material must of necessity appeal to a mass audience, with all that that implies. However, pressure on air-time means that a wide range of subjects will be covered only superficially in small, widely dispersed segments over a weekly schedule.

Broad-based general entertainment channels are the foundation of all national television services, but, in order to appeal to the

Programming

majority of their audience as much of the time as possible, their output must appeal to a notional 'average', or middle-of-the-road taste. In many cases this produces a bland pot-pourri that is designed, more often than not, to offend or frustrate as few people as possible. National broadcasting is the equivalent of being a jack of all trades, while parallel programming is the opportunity for a programme provider to become the master of one!

Advertisers tend to like this kind of approach, as it allows them to target campaigns directly at interested groups of individuals whose tastes and habits can be accurately defined. Relatively small audiences mean that air-time will be considerably cheaper than on the mass-entertainment channels, making it a very cost-effective medium for advertisers, rather like special-interest magazines. This brings many more companies into the TV advertising net that otherwise could not afford to promote products or services on television. As far as satellite channels are concerned, the footprint covers a far wider area than either terrestrial or cable distribution and, perhaps more importantly, allows advertisers to reach an international audience. The language barrier can be a problem, though channels with multi-language soundtracks overcome this drawback. On the plus side, international audiences appeal to well-known multinational companies that are keen to project their corporate images into as many markets as possible.

For parallel programming to work properly, however, a system needs to carry a large number of channels covering as many areas of interest as possible. In some towns and cities, American cable subscribers can choose from as many as fifty different channels; US TVRO owners may have access to as many as 300 TV channels! The range of subjects is almost limitless, restricted only by legal and moral considerations. It would be impossible to list all of the areas covered in this way, but some typical and popular subjects are: music, religion, ethnic minorities, sport, news, fitness and health, soft-core pornography, international finance, cartoons and current affairs of local interest.

A typical domestic STV system in western Europe is capable of receiving up to twenty structured channels. That figure is slightly misleading in some respects, however, as the total number of channels represents the output from two separate satellites over a period of twenty-four hours. In practice only eight to ten channels are available at any one time, because some programme providers share costs by using a single transponder at different times throughout the day. Furthermore, as many as half of them will be in a foreign language or, worse, completely unwatchable if they are scrambled!

Scrambling and encryption

The possibility of some channels scrambling or encrypting their signals is one of the biggest threats to the development of the satellite television market in Europe. Everyone accepts that STV programmes have to be paid for, but as yet there is no clear consensus among programme providers as to how this will be done. Some programme providers have already scrambled their signals but have used a variety of incompatible systems, leaving the viewer with the possibility of having to buy, hire or lease several different types of decoder.

While STV technology is still relatively new, it is extremely vulnerable to such pressures, and this will inevitably create public suspicion. This is hardly surprising; within the last twenty years there have been a succession of consumer products that, for one reason or another, have failed to gain the kind of market demanded for mass-manufacture, and have ultimately been condemned to obsolescence, leaving in their wake thousands of consumers left high and dry, often with useless equipment.

Programme providers who rely upon paid subscriptions to finance their output naturally regard scrambling as a necessary safeguard to prevent their material from being 'stolen' by

Programming

unauthorized viewers. Scrambling has two main advantages: firstly, it enables programme providers to control strictly the sale or rental of decoding equipment; and secondly, it allows them to produce very accurate audience figures. Apart from its value to potential advertisers, it serves as a useful negotiating tool for the programme providers when purchasing the rights to various programmes.

The technology of scrambling is naturally kept a closely guarded secret. Nevertheless, sales of illicit, or 'bootleg', decoders have become a very lucrative business in the US. Plans for DIY unscramblers have been published in various technical magazines, so it has become increasingly likely that many future transmissions will be 'encrypted' rather than simply scrambled.

The differences between scrambling and encryption are considerable. The most commonly used scrambling systems, such as Oak/Orion, rely on a technique that removes the video signal's synchronization pulses. Further options such as inverting, or 'reversing', the video signal can also be applied. What appears on the screen of a normal television set is usually an unwatchable picture that rolls and flickers. Unscrambling equipment regenerates the synchronization signals from a reference signal that is transmitted in place of the normal 'sync' pulses and presents the TV receiver with a normal signal.

Encryption techniques do not normally involve the transmission of conventionally formulated television signals. Instead the signals are converted to a completely new format, rather like a different transmission standard, akin to systems such as PAL, SECAM or NTSC (National Television Standards Committee; see Glossary), which are the most commonly used terrestrial TV broadcast standards.

MAC

The most likely encryption system to be used for STV applications comes under the general heading of MAC, or multiplexed analogue component. A number of variants have been developed, including B-MAC, C-MAC and D2-MAC, each incompatible with the other but offering a distinct advantage or suitability for a particular application.

The MAC system was developed specifically to combat problems with noise and interference that can be troublesome with current TV transmission systems. In particular natural and man-made noise can be particularly disruptive on the high frequencies used for STV transmissions. MAC is an entirely new transmission standard and, unlike previous TV systems, has been developed without the constraints imposed by the need to retain compatibility with existing TV receivers. It is likely that all future TV receivers will have MAC decoders built in during manufacture.

B-MAC and D2-MAC are the frontrunners for future European STV systems, and D2-MAC in particular appears to fit in neatly with future plans for high-definition television. One major advantage of some MAC systems is their 'addressability'. During manufacture each decoder is assigned a unique code number. This enables the programme provider to contact individually each decoder by sending a coded transmission inside the television signals to switch decoders on or off, depending on whether or not the appropriate subscription has been paid or not.

Further enhancements already well past the development stage point to television receivers with built-in magnetic card readers. These could be used directly by the viewer to pay for television programmes, on a pay-per-view basis. Again MAC technology will be used to prevent unauthorized reception of signals.

Unlike scrambling, encryption systems can be virtually uncrackable. Some MAC systems could be likened to a telephone conversation where the sender changes from one language to another every tenth word. Even if it were possible to design and build a decoder to translate, say one language, by the time it had succeeded the language would have changed. MAC can and will be defeated by determined pirates, but its backers are confident that it will allow them to retain the edge for some time to come. It has been estimated that to do so with current technology would work out several thousand times more expensive than any foreseeable subscription fee. How long it will stay that way remains to be seen.

The choice of channels

It is clear that the number of STV channels will increase dramatically over the next ten to fifteen years, but at the moment the choice of eight to ten channels from Intelsat V-FII and ECS-FI is more than enough for most normal people. (To that figure must be added any locally available terrestrial channels.) Even seemingly unintelligible foreign-language channels can be fascinating to watch, especially the advertisements. More importantly, however, they are potentially a very useful tool for language students – an ideal way to keep up to date with current usage (and abusage).

The following is a brief run-down of channels available over western Europe from ECS-FI and Intelsat V-FII at the time of writing.

The Arts Channel

The Arts Channel operates for an average of three hours each day between 6.00 and 9.00 every morning. Topics covered include classical music, opera, drama, visual arts and inverviews with personalities. The Arts Channel is primarily intended for distribution to cable networks. Programmes are recorded on video tape for screening later in the day.

Business Television Network (BTN)

BTN is a daily summary of the international financial market, broadcast from the US every evening. BTN includes programming provided by the American cable station Financial News Network (FNN) and the *Wall Street Journal*.

Cable News Network (CNN)

CNN was the first round-the-clock news service. It originates from the US and is intended mainly for distribution to the European hotel market. Programming is slick and well presented. CNN assumes that viewers will watch only for relatively short periods throughout the day; hence the 'rolling news' format that results in a fair amount of repetition during any period of twenty-four hours.

The Children's Channel

The Children's Channel, as its name suggests, is aimed directly at children and teenagers, with a mixture of cartoons, films, magazine programmes and puppet shows.

Europa Television

Europa is the newest of the STV channels. It is currently transmitted with an English-language soundtrack, although there are plans to add other languages on separate audio channels later this year. Programme content is fairly broad, with concentration on news, current affairs and cultural programmes of interest to a pan-European audience.

Filmnet

The Dutch/Belgian ATN Filmnet carries a wide range of popular, classic and recently released feature films, mostly with an original English-language soundtrack but always with Dutch/Flemish subtitles. The schedule includes around twenty or so new films each month, repeated an average of four times over a four-week period. The Filmnet signal is now scrambled, although decoders are available to subscribing individuals.

Lifestyle

Lifestyle, operated by W. H. Smith & Sons Television Services, provides a daytime schedule centred around a wide selection of 'women's interest' material. This includes features and programmes on cookery, fashion, health and home finance, as well as soap operas. Programmes are drawn from a variety of sources and include archive material such as the *Galloping Gourmet*, and the American *Doctor Ruth Show*, a controversial sex-therapy phone-in.

Premiere

Premiere shares the same transponder as the Children's Channel. Output consists of a mixture of cinema and made-for-TV films plus early evening cartoons and soaps. Around twenty new films are added each month and generally repeated three or four times over a thirty-day period.

RAI-Uno

RAI-Uno is the Italian, state-operated general entertainment channel. RAI is primarily intended for distribution to isolated communities within Italy that cannot receive normal terrestrial broadcasts. Programme material is in Italian and includes a fair proportion of sport (mainly football), music shows, news and current affairs. RAI is very popular with expatriate Italians throughout Europe.

RTL-Plus

RTL originates in Luxembourg and carries mainly German general entertainment, news and current-affairs programmes.

Sat-1

Sat-1 is a general entertainment channel carrying a wide variety of news, sport, music and current affairs.

Screen Sport

Screen Sport, managed by W. H. Smith & Sons Cable Television Services, transmits an average of eight hours each day. Programme content, not surprisingly, is sports orientated. Much of the material is drawn from American sources and contains a proportion of specialist sports (e.g. professional arm-wrestling!) as well as more mainstream interests such as football, motor racing, basketball and even fishing.

Sky Channel

Sky was one of the very first channels specifically designed for transmission to European cable networks via satellite links. Sky is not generally available to individual TVRO owners and is scrambled using the Oak/Orion system. Decoders are available at a cost of around £400 to two or more subscribers sharing a common aerial system. Programme content is largely based on American-made soaps, cartoons, serials and comedy shows.

Superchannel

Superchannel transmits a 24-hour schedule, consisting of material drawn mainly from the BBC and IBA archives. Ten hours of the schedule (midnight to 6.00 a.m. and 6.00 to 7.00 p.m.) are taken up by Music Box, a programme and production company; hour-long pop video compilations, chart shows and interviews with personalities, along with news and magazine features, are presented by a team of 'veejays'. Weekend programming includes 'in-concert' material featuring top-name bands and artists.

Teleclub

Teleclub, the Swiss-based general entertainment channel, transmits mostly German-language material and top-name feature films (dubbed into German).

TV5

TV5 is a French-language general entertainment channel, transmitted in SECAM. On normal UK television receivers this results in a monochrome picture. Programme content is broad-based, with a fair number of music and light entertainment shows.

Chapter 5: Space hardware

The simplest way to sum up the vast amount of technology and the myriad of operations carried out by communications satellites is to think of them as remotely controlled mirrors. Signals are beamed up to the satellite from ground-based earth stations; the satellite then picks up the signals, amplifies them and beams them back to earth in a precise pattern, using steerable, parabolic dish antennae. Communications satellites are designed to work with a variety of signal formats, provided that they fulfil specified engineering parameters. This gives them an enormous degree of flexibility, and a typical communications satellite can handle a tremendous mixture of signals: a single transponder might carry 1,000 telephone circuits or a video signal with five audio channels. As far as the satellite is concerned, the content and purpose of the transmission is irrelevant; only its origin and destination are important.

It is all too easy to ignore the fantastic technology involved in communications satellites; they are completely invisible from Earth, and, once operational, they rarely appear to go wrong. In fact, setting a satellite into orbit in the first place is the biggest hurdle and the statistics clearly indicate that the first few seconds of a satellite's journey are the most hazardous.

No launch vehicle yet built can get a satellite from the Earth directly into a geostationary orbit. While technically feasible, this

Space hardware

would be an extremely wasteful and expensive exercise. In practice the insertion into orbit is made in several stages, depending upon the type of vehicle used.

Until very recently the Americans had a virtual monopoly on commercial satellite launchers with the reusable Shuttle orbiter system and several types of heavy boosters, mostly developed for military applications. These include Atlas, Centaur, Thor and Titan rockets – all relatively reliable in the highly unpredictable world of rocketry but now widely regarded as almost obsolete and highly inefficient.

Shuttle was conceived in the wake of the Apollo moon programme as a general-purpose, reusable launch system. Financial constraints imposed before, during and after development meant that its eventual operational characteristics fell far short of the original specifications. Shuttle was designed to be a multi-role civilian and military system, one that would keep America and, more pertinently, NASA in space until the turn of the century. In the event, severe cutbacks, mainly in rocket motor capacity, have left Shuttle with a limited capability that restricts it to a low-altitude orbit and the somewhat worrying prospect of unpowered, 'dead stick' landings.

Shuttle is unable to reach the high orbits needed by geosynchronous satellites. Instead they are catapulted from the orbiter's cargo bay and pushed into a higher orbit by a small booster rocket strapped to the underside of the satellite.

The European Space Agency's Ariane launcher was developed in roughly the same timespan as Shuttle but was primarily a civilian project, designed from the outset to carry commercial payloads. Ariane has had its fair share of failures but is now widely accepted as a reliable system. The eventual intention is for Ariane to be 'man-rated', and plans are well advanced for a reusable 'mini-shuttle' space plane that will sit atop Ariane 5 boosters.

The destruction of the Shuttle Challenger and the tragic death of its crew of seven in 1986 was quickly followed by a number of well-publicized failures of unmanned launch vehicles (including one Ariane launcher). Those events effectively shattered the once complacent attitudes held by the Americans, and their unchallenged superiority in space came to an abrupt halt. In the wake of the Challenger disaster, Ariane was joined by a number of launchers available to carry commercial payloads, notably from countries such as Japan and China. There is even a remote possibility that one day Russian rockets will carry commercial payloads, although at the time of writing this was still far from certain.

Firing orders

Getting one or more satellites into geostationary orbit usually involves a number of well-defined stages, beginning with the actual take-off. This is the most hazardous part of a spacecraft's journey, not only because of the risk of explosion, but also because of the tremendously high levels of mechanical vibration which, if unchecked, could rapidly reduce a delicate communications satellite to a worthless pile of junk.

The first stage of a launcher rocket is usually exhausted within a few minutes of take-off, hurling the vehicle a few tens of miles from the launch pad. The empty tanks and expended rocket motors are jettisoned, and once they are clear of the rocket the craft's second stage ignites; this will propel the craft to an altitude of around 140 miles above the Earth's surface. The third-stage rockets take over to push the vehicle into an elliptically shaped transfer orbit that takes the craft out to its 'parking orbit' at its furthest point (apogee) and back close to the Earth (perigee).

When conditions are correct, an instruction from the control centre on Earth fires a small rocket motor to take the satellite away from the launch vehicle and accelerate it up to the 6,900 mph required to keep it in geostationary orbit. Once the satellite is in its correct orbital position, the solar panels are deployed to provide power for all of the satellite's electrical and electronic systems. The panels extend from the body of the craft on long delicate booms and are kept facing the sun by small, automatically activated servo motors.

With the solar panels extended, the satellite becomes operational, and there is normally a 'shakedown' period while engineers on Earth check out the satellite's functions before it is fully commissioned. In the event of a system or circuit failing, ground engineers can normally switch in back-up circuitry to keep the craft fully operational – the cost, uncertainties and lack of repair facilities in space mean that there is almost always provision for 'redundancy' in critical systems. This does not apply only to the post-launch shakedown period: there will be failures and faults throughout a satellite's operational life, so it is important to ensure that no one failure could ruin the whole system's operational capability.

In principle, a satellite in geostationary orbit will remain in position indefinitely; the frictionless vacuum of space and the finely counterbalanced effects of gravity and centrifugal force should, in theory at least, ensure that it stays put. In practice a variety of forces act upon satellites, causing them to go 'walkabout'. Major influences include solar winds emanating from the sun and variations in gravitational pull from the Earth, moon, sun and nearby planets.

Geostationary satellites have to be repositioned once every two months on average. Each satellite is allotted a precise orbital position by international agreement; in the case of communications satellites, this is defined most easily as the centre of a square some 70 miles across. Satellite operators usually attempt to keep the satellite to within 20 metres of its nominal position with the use of miniature rocket motors, or 'puffers', using a chemical fuel known as hydrazine. Station-keeping motors, controlled from an earth station, develop an extremely small thrust, around one-tenth of a pound. That contrasts strongly with an orbital transfer rocket motor, which typically produces up to 50,000 pounds of thrust, and the Shuttle's main boosters, which develop a staggering seven million pounds!

While it would be possible to build larger station-keeping rockets into a satellite, these would be undesirable. The effect of a more powerful thrust could literally tear the satellite apart. Although relatively sturdy during the launch phase, a satellite becomes extremely fragile once the solar panels are deployed, and any subsequent movement must be slow and finely controlled to prevent damage. Very small changes in a satellite's attitude can be effected using gyroscopic devices; these are electrically operated and do not rely on precious rocket fuel.

Weight restrictions and the inaccessibility of geostationary orbits prevent satellites from being refuelled, so the hydrazine carried at take-off has to last for the satellite's operational life. The current average life expectancy for a communications satellite is around seven years, by which time the fuel will have been exhausted and some electronic components and systems will be nearing the end of their projected lives. Normally the last few pounds of fuel are used to propel the satellite out of the Earth's orbit in order to make room for a replacement.

Some attempts have been made to recover redundant or malfunctioning satellites, although the only successful missions so far have been with satellites that failed to reach their correct orbit and could be recovered manually by astronauts operating from the Shuttle's low earth orbit.

Power problems

All of the satellite's electrical power has to come from the solar panels. The exception is during periods of an Earth eclipse, when the Earth comes between the satellite and the sun, thus putting the panels into shadow. Fortunately eclipses of this kind are most common in the spring and occur only when the area covered by the

Space hardware

satellite's footprint is in darkness; coincidentally, these tend to occur late at night or early in the morning, during periods of relative inactivity, at least as far as TV broadcasting is concerned. However, most current satellites carry telecommunications traffic as well as some TV channels. When the solar panels are in darkness, banks of nickel cadmium (nicad) rechargeable batteries are used to keep the satellite operational.

Satellites come in numerous shapes and sizes, and are designed to fulfil specific applications that may range from scientific survey and weather observation to less well-publicized military or intelligence activities. However, the ones used to carry television signals share a number of common features, the most notable being the parabolic dish antennae used to transmit the signals back down to Earth. Normally, each of the transponder antennae is steerable, to allow the ground operators to aim the transmissions accurately over an area of the Earth's surface. In practice the antennae will be held to within one-tenth of a degree. Similarly, the receiving antennae pointing at a satellite must be aligned to within one-half of a degree to ensure maximum signal strength.

Although the power generated by a satellite's solar-panel array is relatively small, the concentrated transmission patterns produced by the spacecraft's dish antennae are equivalent in coverage to earth-bound transmitters operating at power levels running into hundreds of thousands of watts. The concept of an 'effective' radiated power (EIRP) of a satellite transmitter bears close comparison to a small light bulb. Simply hung from its wires, the light would, perhaps, be visible over a few tens of metres in any direction. If the bulb is then mounted at the focal point of a parabolic mirror, the concentrated beam of light would then be visible from several hundreds, even thousands of metres away – but from only one point in the light beam's path. To produce the same effect with a bulb without a reflector would involve using a light source many thousands of times larger and more powerful than a torch bulb.

The next generation of DBS satellites will employ similar technology to existing communications satellites. DBS spacecraft are designed primarily for television broadcasting rather than telecommunications, so transmission power will be increased by a factor of twenty to thirty times that currently used. This will allow much smaller receiving antennae to be used that are typically 90 centimetres in diameter. The rest of the viewer's equipment, however, will remain largely the same, apart from the possible need to incorporate additional unscrambling equipment within the system. If unscramblers do come into use, they will simply plug into existing receivers.

Chapter 6: Implications

Few developments in the history of evolution have had such far-reaching effects in such a short space of time as satellite communications; yet most of us are completely unaware of the role that they are playing in all of our lives and, more importantly, the possibilities for good and ill that may lie in store for future generations. It is becoming clear that we are still only at the very beginning of a wholly new era in our development, one that is possibly more far-reaching in its implications than the combined effects of the Iron and Bronze ages and the Industrial Revolution.

Satellites carry images and voices from the remotest corners of this planet into our living-rooms. Television pictures from around the world can alert us to national and international events: war, famine and catastrophe appear to us even as they happen. News of man-made and natural disasters can be flashed across continents in seconds, bringing in their wake national and international rescue efforts and relief worth millions of pounds. Huge sums of money can be collected in a matter of hours; this is possible only with the aid of satellite technology.

It would be easy to be cynical about the attendant publicity afforded by television under such circumstances, and the sometimes questionable motives of governments, relief organizations and individuals, but the indisputable fact remains that but for this sort of television coverage, many thousands, possibly millions, of people would almost certainly have died.

On a more mundane, though no less worthy level, satellite television is drawing us, as a species, just a little closer together. It gives individuals unprecedented access to television programming from other countries around the world. While the more sinister applications of this type of cross-frontier broadcasting have not gone unnoticed by propagandists, STV could one day give millions of people an insight into their neighbours' lives. We tend to fear what we do not understand; perhaps the knowledge that one nation's game shows are as dreadful as our own, or that they have the same problems in getting their whites whiter, will make them seem less threatening?

Even if STV does become an instrument of propaganda (and human nature being what it is, that is inevitable), the sheer diversity of material that will be available from all persuasions should go some way towards cancelling out some of the more extreme viewpoints, giving the viewer a greater pool of opinion from which to choose.

Satellite television is proving to be a powerful educational tool in the Third World. Countries too poor to afford full-scale national television networks can now look to STV to provide the kind of coverage that in the past would have required thousands of costly land-based transmitters. Countries such as India have conducted successful experiments with satellite distribution of educational programmes, mainly to isolated communities and villages. The cost of leasing transponders on existing satellites, maintaining an earth station and providing receiving equipment works out at a fraction of the price of a network of terrestrial transmitters. Moreover, it is a flexible option that does not require a vast capital outlay in hardware and can be altered or tailored to suit the prevailing needs.

Satellite technology has touched the lives of almost everyone on this planet – even those without televisions. Anyone within reach of a telephone now has access to an international telecommunications network that reaches approximately one-third of the world's population. Communications in the wider sense now extend far beyond two-way telephone conversations; today much of the international telecommunications traffic is in the form of electronic computer data. Governments, multinational corporations and even individuals use satellite-borne computer and telex links to keep in touch with each other. Armies and navies also rely on satellite technology in ways that extend far beyond mere communications. Aside from their more sensitive applications in surveillance, satellites now provide global navigational information. Receiving equipment fitted to ships and aircraft can give highly accurate location fixes, and plans for portable satellite navigation receivers are already well advanced. One day it may be possible to install such equipment into a family motorcar.

What of the television picture of the future? It is possible that satellite television will provide the necessary impetus for a completely new standard in TV broadcasting.

The picture quality of contemporary television receivers is generally very good, although by comparison with optical or photographic film (such as the 35mm film used in most cinemas) the very distinct 'grain' of a TV picture and the slight amount of flickering is noticeable. In addition the aspect ratio of a TV picture, which is defined as the relationship of the screen's height to its width, gives it an almost square appearance. A normal television screen has an aspect ratio of 3:4, that is, three units high by four units wide. This contrasts with a typical cinema screen, which has an aspect ratio of 3:5, giving a far wider screen area that better fills the viewer's field of vision. These two deficiencies have been largely overcome with a number of developments; these are jointly referred to under the heading of 'high-definition television', or HDTV.

Several HDTV systems have been developed by manufacturers and broadcasting organizations around the world to the stage where mass production could easily be implemented. However, there are enormous costs involved in re-equipping studios and establishing transmission facilities, and for production costs to be low enough for a mass-market there would have to be one world market using one internationally agreed standard or format. As yet no one system has received enough endorsements to establish the new standard.

Whichever system is ultimately adopted, though, it is unlikely that HDTV broadcasts will ever utilize ground-based transmitters. Apart from being tied up during the phasing-out period of ten to twenty years for current technologies, there simply will not be enough space on the already overcrowded radio broadcast spectrum to allow for these new signals. HDTV images are composed of over 1,000 picture lines,* so that the grain is removed. In effect, the signal will be far more complex than a conventional TV signal, and will occupy a larger segment of the radio spectrum. It is therefore probable that satellite channels, which do not suffer from the same degree of overcrowding, will be set aside for these transmissions.

The net result of HDTV is a television picture that is virtually indistinguishable from a photograph. Screens with aspect ratios of 3:5 or greater will reinforce the wide-screen cinematic impression, and these features, coupled with high-fidelity surround sound, will almost certainly herald a new era in television entertainment.

These are just some of the possibilities that could be opened up by satellite technology within the next decade. But what of the more distant future – how will these developments affect our lives in the next century and where will they ultimately lead? Clearly, it is impossible to tell, but perhaps now is the time for us to take stock and try to influence the shape of the future. Now is the time

---

* Each television picture, or 'frame', on current PAL, SECAM or NTSC TVs is built up from hundreds of horizontal lines that go to make up a single, still picture. Each frame lasts for only one-fiftieth of a second (1/60th of a second on NTSC), but an effect known as persistence of vision fools the human eye into seeing what looks like a moving picture rather than a series of still photographs.

Implications

to make the decisions that will direct this powerful technology. Unless the correct decisions are made right now, the technology will dictate its own course – a mistake that has happened all too frequently in the past.

In the wrong hands satellite communications, indeed, any form of communications, can be a weapon of terrifying proportions; in the right hands it can be a tool that will benefit us all. Those who control it wield unimaginable power for good or evil. Ever since the first Soviet and American satellites were launched in the late 1950s, the military colonization of space has been a real and terrifying prospect. More recently it has become the centre of a new debate with the advent of the US's proposed Strategic Defense Initiative (SDI), more popularly known as the 'Star Wars' plan. This almost inconceivable new twist in the saga proposes that the Earth should be encircled with a variety of weapons designed to eliminate intercontinental missiles before they get a chance to reach their target. Counter measures developed by the Soviet Union include 'hunter-killer' satellites packed with high explosives, designed to track down and destroy enemy satellites. At the moment, at least, the technology on both sides appears to be some way from becoming a practical reality. However, the implications are clear: space could become the first, and probably the last, battlefield of the twenty-first century. Let us hope that good sense will prevail . . .

In the meantime, and on a less serious note, satellite technology is here, right now, to entertain and inform us. Within ten years home satellite dishes will be as commonplace as washing machines, and probably just about as interesting. *Now* is the most exciting time in this rapidly developing technology – try it before it's too late . . .

Appendices

Appendix 1: Domestic satellite systems for under £1,500

Avitel AV850

Receiver

Type:	set-top
Tuning:	manual/rotary
Controls:	polarity
Remote control:	no

Dish

Diameter (metres):	1.2
Style:	parabolic offset
Mount:	elaz

Actuators

Motor drive:	optional
Polarator:	optional

Avitel AV1000

Receiver
Type: set-top
Tuning: push-button
Controls: polarity, antenna alignment
Remote control: yes

Dish

Diameter (metres): 1.2
Style: parabolic offset
Mount: elaz

Actuators

Motor drive: optional
Polarator: optional

Bel Micro-Eye

Receiver

Type: set-top
Tuning: push-button
Controls: polarity, antenna alignment
Remote control: yes

Dish

Diameter (metres): 1.5
Style: one-piece parabolic
Mount: polar

Actuators

Motor drive: optional
Polarator: optional

The Beginner's Guide to Satellite TV

Comex TVRO Kit

Receiver

Type:	DIY kit
Tuning:	manual/rotary
Controls:	polarity, video invert
Remote control:	no

Dish

Diameter (metres):	N/A
Style:	N/A
Mount:	N/A

Actuators

Motor drive:	N/A
Polarator:	N/A

Connexions CX2450

Receiver

Type:	set-top
Tuning:	manual/rotary
Controls:	polarity
Remote control:	no

Dish

Diameter (metres):	1.2
Style:	parabolic offset
Mount:	elaz

Actuators

Motor drive:	optional
Polarator:	optional

Appendices

Connexions CX245R

Receiver

Type: set-top
Tuning: push-button
Controls: polarity
Remote control: yes

Dish

Diameter (metres): 1.2
Style: parabolic offset
Mount: elaz

Actuators

Motor drive: optional
Polarator: optional

Echosphere SR-1000

Receiver

Type: set-top
Tuning: manual/rotary
Controls: polarity
Remote control: no

Dish

Diameter (metres): 1.5
Style: one-piece parabolic
Mount: elaz

Actuators

Motor drive: optional
Polarator: optional

Echosphere SR-3000

Receiver

Type:	set-top
Tuning:	push-button
Controls:	polarity, antenna alignment
Remote control:	yes

Dish

Diameter (metres):	1.5
Style:	one-piece parabolic
Mount:	polar

Actuators

Motor drive:	optional
Polarator:	optional

Ferguson ES01

Receiver

Type:	set-top
Tuning:	push-button
Controls:	polarity
Remote control:	yes

Dish

Diameter (metres):	1.5
Style:	one-piece parabolic
Mount:	polar

Actuators

Motor drive:	optional
Polarator:	optional

Appendices

Ferguson ES02

Receiver

Type:	set-top
Tuning:	push-button
Controls:	polarity
Remote control:	yes

Dish

Diameter (metres):	1.8
Style:	one-piece parabolic
Mount:	polar

Actuators

Motor drive:	optional
Polarator:	optional

Grundig STR 200

Receiver

Type:	set-top
Tuning:	push-button
Controls:	polarity
Remote control:	yes

Dish

Diameter (metres):	1.5
Style:	one-piece parabolic
Mount:	polar

Actuators

Motor drive:	optional
Polarator:	optional

The Beginner's Guide to Satellite TV

Handic 5000

Receiver

Type: set-top
Tuning: manual/rotary
Controls: polarity
Remote control: no

Dish

Diameter (metres): 1.5
Style: one-piece parabolic
Mount: elaz

Actuators

Motor drive: no
Polarator: no

ITT Digivision DR1

Receiver

Type: set-top
Tuning: push-button
Controls: polarity, antenna alignment
Remote control: yes

Dish

Diameter (metres): 1.4
Style: square offset parabolic
Mount: polar

Actuators

Motor drive: optional
Polarator: optional

Lenson Heath LH3000

Receiver

Type:	set-top
Tuning:	manual
Controls:	polarity
Remote control:	no

Dish

Diameter (metres):	1.8
Style:	parabolic petalized
Mount:	elaz

Actuators

Motor drive:	optional
Polarator:	optional

Luxor 3000

Receiver

Type:	set-top
Tuning:	push-button
Controls:	polarity
Remote control:	no

Dish

Diameter (metres):	1.5
Style:	one-piece parabolic
Mount:	elaz

Actuators

Motor drive:	no
Polarator:	optional

Luxor 5000

Receiver

Type:	built into TV receiver
Tuning:	push-button
Controls:	video invert
Remote control:	yes (TV set)

Dish

Diameter (metres):	1.5
Style:	one-piece parabolic
Mount:	elaz

Actuators

Motor drive:	no
Polarator:	optional

Maspro SRE800S

Receiver

Type:	set-top
Tuning:	manual/rotary
Controls:	polarity
Remote control:	no

Dish

Diameter (metres):	1.2
Style:	parabolic offset
Mount:	elaz

Actuators

Motor drive:	optional
Polarator:	optional

Megasat Patio Pack

Receiver

Type:	set-top
Tuning:	manual/rotary
Controls:	polarity
Remote control:	no

Dish

Diameter (metres):	1.8
Style:	one-piece parabolic
Mount:	elaz

Actuators

Motor drive:	optional
Polarator:	optional

Multipoint MRS11

Receiver

Type:	set-top
Tuning:	push-button
Controls:	polarity
Remote control:	no

Dish

Diameter (metres):	1.8
Style:	one-piece parabolic
Mount:	elaz

Actuators

Motor drive:	optional
Polarator:	optional

NEC 1022

Receiver

Type:	set-top
Tuning:	push-button
Controls:	polarity
Remote control:	no

Dish

Diameter (metres):	1.8
Style:	one-piece parabolic
Mount:	elaz

Actuators

Motor drive:	optional
Polarator:	optional

NEC 2022

Receiver

Type:	set-top
Tuning:	push-button
Controls:	polarity
Remote control:	yes

Dish

Diameter (metres):	1.2 to 1.8
Style:	one-piece parabolic
Mount:	polar

Actuators

Motor drive:	optional
Polarator:	yes

Appendices

Network

Receiver

Type:	set-top
Tuning:	manual/rotary
Controls:	polarity
Remote control:	no

Dish

Diameter (metres):	1.6
Style:	one-piece parabolic
Mount:	elaz

Actuators

Motor drive:	optional
Polarator:	optional

Orbitel ORBI

Receiver

Type:	set-top
Tuning	manual/rotary
Controls:	polarity
Remote control:	no

Dish

Diameter (metres):	1.8
Style:	one-piece parabolic
Mount:	elaz

Actuators

Motor drive:	no
Polarator:	optional

Orbitel ORB2

Receiver

Type:	set-top
Tuning:	manual
Controls:	polarity
Remote control:	no

Dish

Diameter (metres):	1.8
Style:	one-piece parabolic
Mount:	elaz

Actuators

Motor drive:	optional
Polarator:	yes

Orbitel ORB3

Receiver

Type:	set-top
Tuning:	manual/rotary
Controls:	polarity
Remote control:	yes

Dish

Diameter (metres):	1.8
Style:	one-piece parabolic
Mount:	elaz

Actuators

Motor drive:	optional
Polarator:	yes

Appendices

Orbitel ORB4

Receiver

Type:	set-top
Tuning:	manual/rotary
Controls:	polarity, antenna alignment
Remote control:	yes

Dish

Diameter (metres):	1.8
Style:	one-piece parabolic
Mount:	polar

Actuators

Motor drive:	yes
Polarator:	yes

Philips SA-100

Receiver

Type:	set-top
Tuning:	push-button
Controls:	polarity
Remote control:	yes

Dish

Diameter (metres):	1.8
Style:	one-piece petalized
Mount:	polar

Actuators

Motor drive:	optional
Polarator:	optional

The Beginner's Guide to Satellite TV

Rediffusion Sat-Pack

Receiver

Type:	set-top
Tuning:	push-button
Controls:	N/A
Remote control:	yes

Dish

Diameter (metres):	1.2
Style:	one-piece parabolic
Mount:	elaz

Actuators

Motor drive:	no
Polarator:	no

Salora SRVII

Receiver

Type:	set-top
Tuning:	push-button
Controls:	polarity
Remote control:	no

Dish

Diameter (metres):	1.5
Style:	one-piece parabolic
Mount:	elaz

Actuators

Motor drive:	no
Polarator:	optional

Appendices

Salora 6190

Receiver

Type:	built into TV receiver
Tuning:	push-button
Controls:	polarity
Remote control:	yes (via TV)

Dish

Diameter (metres):	1.5
Style:	one-piece parabolic
Mount:	elaz

Actuators

Motor drive:	no
Polarator:	optional

Sat-Tel STR1

Receiver

Type:	set-top
Tuning:	push-button
Controls:	polarity
Remote control:	no

Dish

Diameter (metres):	1.8
Style:	one-piece parabolic
Mount:	elaz

Actuators

Motor drive:	optional
Polarator:	optional

Satvrn TDM 1220

Receiver

Type:	set-top
Tuning:	push-button
Controls:	polarity
Remote control:	yes

Dish

Diameter (metres):	1.8
Style:	one-piece parabolic
Mount:	polar

Actuators

Motor drive:	optional
Polarator:	optional

Skyscan K1

Receiver

Type:	set-top
Tuning:	push-button
Controls:	polarity, antenna alignment
Remote control:	yes

Dish

Diameter (metres):	1.5
Style:	parabolic offset
Mount:	polar

Actuators

Motor drive:	yes
Polarator:	yes

Appendices

STS 304

Receiver

Type:	set-top
Tuning:	push-button
Controls:	polarity
Remote control:	no

Dish

Diameter (metres):	1.2
Style:	parabolic offset
Mount:	elaz

Actuators

Motor drive:	optional
Polarator:	optional

STS 304P

Receiver

Type:	set-top
Tuning:	push-button
Controls:	polarity
Remote control:	no

Dish

Diameter (metres):	1.2
Style:	parabolic offset
Mount:	elaz

Actuators

Motor drive:	optional
Polarator:	yes

STS 304PH

Receiver

Type: set-top
Tuning: push-button
Controls: polarity
Remote control: no

Dish

Diameter (metres): 1.2
Style: parabolic offset
Mount: polar

Actuators

Motor drive: optional
Polarator: yes

STS 304PM

Receiver

Type: set-top
Tuning: push-button
Controls: polarity, antenna alignment
Remote control: no

Dish

Diameter (metres): 1.2
Style: parabolic offset
Mount: polar

Actuators

Motor drive: yes
Polarator: yes

Appendices

Telsat PR4001

Receiver

Type:	set-top
Tuning:	push-button
Controls:	polarity
Remote control:	no

Dish

Diameter (metres):	1.8
Style:	one-piece parabolic
Mount:	elaz

Actuators

Motor drive:	no
Polarator:	no

Tratec A1000

Receiver

Type:	set-top
Tuning:	push-button
Controls:	polarity, antenna alignment
Remote control:	yes

Dish

Diameter (metres):	N/A
Style:	N/A
Mount:	N/A

Actuators

Motor drive:	N/A
Polarator:	N/A

The Beginner's Guide to Satellite TV

Uniace UST-3000

Receiver

Type:	set-top
Tuning:	push-button
Controls:	polarity
Remote control:	no

Dish

Diameter (metres):	1.7
Style:	one-piece parabolic
Mount:	elaz

Actuators

Motor drive:	optional
Polarator:	optional

Vusat Sat 100

Receiver

Type:	set-top
Tuning:	push-button
Controls:	polarity
Remote control:	yes

Dish

Diameter (metres):	1.2
Style:	parabolic offset
Mount:	elaz

Actuators

Motor drive:	optional
Polarator:	yes

Appendix 2: Technical data and addresses

Antenna alignment data for ECS-F1 and Intelsat V-F11

Eutelsat ECS-F1

Location	Azimuth	Elevation
South coast	161.6	30.1
London	163.5	29.8
Midlands	161.4	28.4
North	161.3	27.2
Border	168.2	25.7
Highlands	162.2	23.5

Intelsat V-F11

Location	Azimuth	Elevation
South coast	213.6	26.7
London	213.6	25.7
Midlands	211.2	25.4
North	210.4	24.5
Borders	208.6	22.7
Highlands	209.4	21.2

Positional data for European STV satellites

Arabsat

Orbital position: 19 degrees east
Frequencies: C-band

The Beginner's Guide to Satellite TV

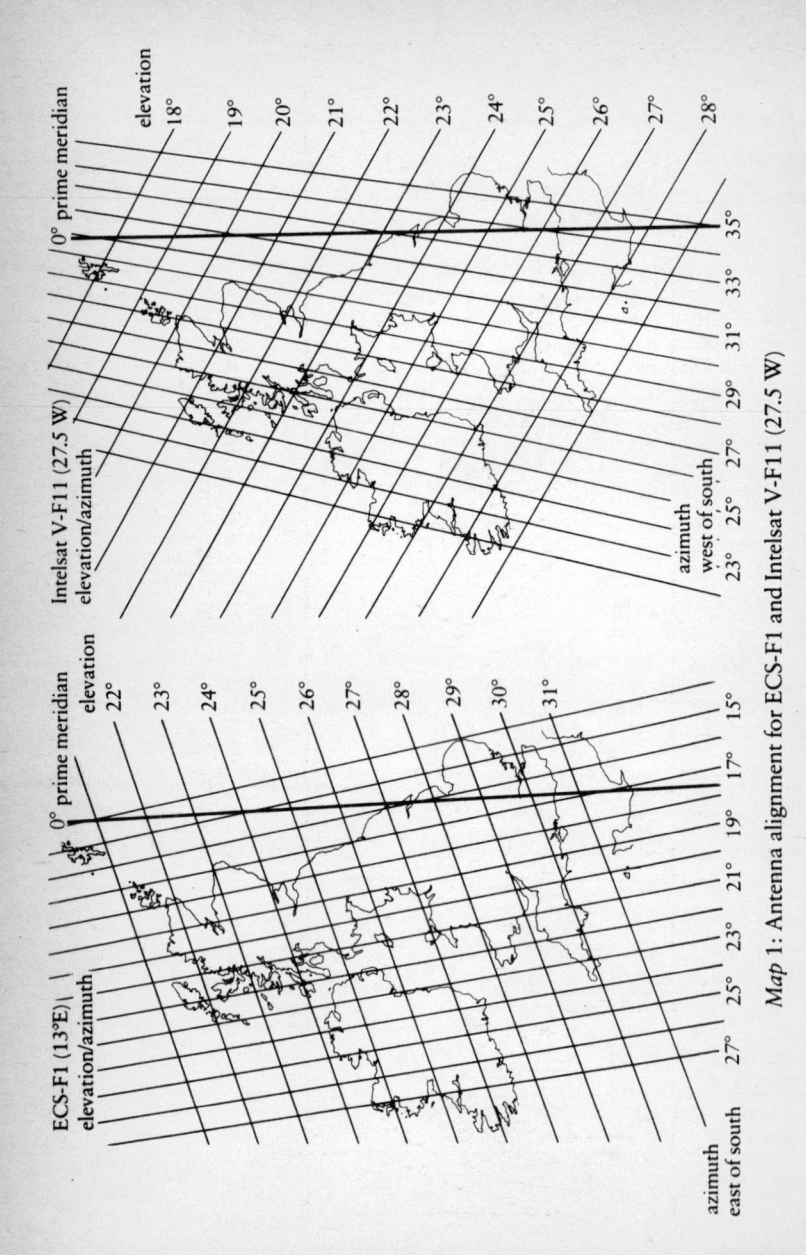

Map 1: Antenna alignment for ECS-F1 and Intelsat V-F11 (27.5 W)

92

Appendices

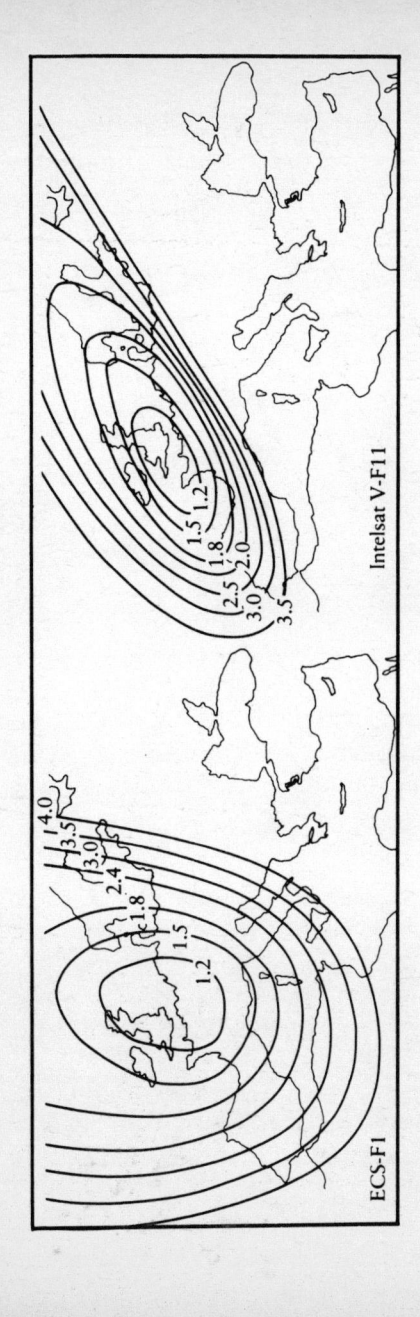

Map 2: Footprints of ECS-F1 and Intelsat V-F11 (27.5 W). Contour lines show areas of equal signal strength; figures show approximate minimum diameter of dish antennae in metres

The Beginner's Guide to Satellite TV

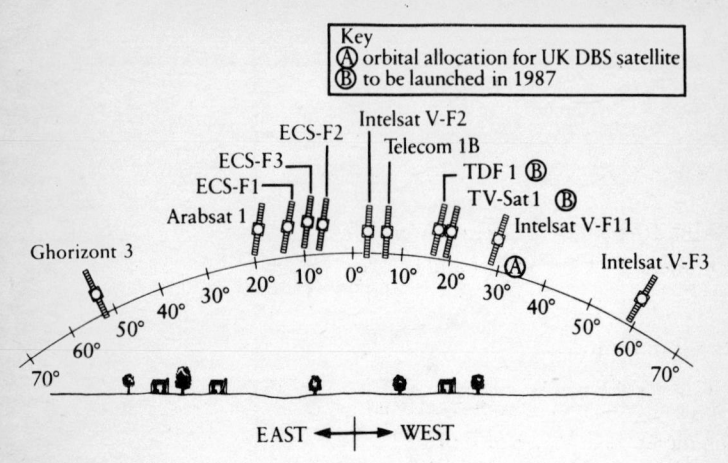

> Key
> Ⓐ orbital allocation for UK DBS satellite
> Ⓑ to be launched in 1987

Map 3: View of the Clarke Belt, looking south

ECS-F1

Orbital position: 13 degrees east
Frequencies: KU-band

ECS-F2

Orbital position: 7 degrees east
Frequencies: KU-band

ECS-F3

Orbital position: 10 degrees east
Frequencies: KU-band

Appendices

Ghorizont 3

Orbital position: 53 degrees east
Frequencies: C-band

Intelsat V-F2

Orbital position: 1 degree west
Frequencies: KU-band

Intelsat V-F3

Orbital position: 60 degrees east
Frequencies: KU-band

Intelsat V-F11

Orbital position: 27.5 degrees west
Frequencies: KU-band

TDF-1

Orbital position: 19 degrees west
Frequencies: KU-band

Telecom 1B

Orbital position: 5 degrees west
Frequencies: KU-band

TV-Sat

Orbital position: 19 degrees west
Frequencies: KU-band

The Beginner's Guide to Satellite TV

STV manufacturers/distributors

A. J. Smith (Satellite) Ltd
14 Fairways
Pershore
Worcestershire WR10 1HA
Tel: 0386 553285

Armstrong Electronics
4/9 Bessington Court
Dublin 7
Republic of Ireland
Tel: 0001 30922

Avitel Spacenet Corp.
580 Deslauriers Avenue
Montreal
Quebec
Canada H4N 1V8
Tel: 010 1 514 333 5544

B.E.L. Tronics (UK) Ltd
Cherry Orchard North
Kembrey Park Industrial Estate
Swindon
Wiltshire SN2 6BL
Tel: 0793 619100

Comex Systems Ltd
Comex House
Unit 4
Bath Lane
Leicester LE3 5BF
Tel: 0533 25084

Connexions Satellite Systems Ltd
125 East Barnet Road
New Barnet
Hertfordshire EN4 8RF
Tel: 01 441 1282

D.X. Antenna Co. Ltd
Adolf Baeyensstraat 147
B-9110 Ghent
Belgium
Tel: 010 3291 288686

Dynastar Satellite Systems
Unit 16
Shaw Lane Industrial Estate
Wheatley
Doncaster
South Yorkshire DN2 4SE
Tel: 0302 27424

Echosphere Corp.
2500 South Raritan
Englewood
CO 80110
USA
Tel: 010 1 303 934 4484

F.B. Cosmos Parabol Teknik
Box 2049
S-68102
Kristinenhamn
Sweden
Tel: 010 46 550 83350

Ferguson
Thorn EMI Ferguson Ltd
Cambridge House
Great Cambridge Road
Enfield
Middlesex EN1 1UL
Tel: 01 363 5353

General Instrument (UK) Ltd
Jerrold Division
95 Farnham Road
Slough
Berkshire SL1 4UN
Tel: 0753 78051

Greenwich Satellite
Tex House
62–4 Beresford Street
London SE18 6BG
Tel: 01 316 1200

Grundig International Ltd
Mill Road
Rugby
Warwickshire CV21 1PR
Tel: 0788 77155

Handic Satellite (UK)
Victor Technologies (UK) Ltd
Unit 1
Valley Centre
Gordon Road
High Wycombe
Bucks. HP13 6EQ
Tel: 0494 450661

Harrison Electronics
Century Way
March
Cambridgeshire PE15 4QW
Tel: 0354 51289

ITT Consumer Electronics (UK) Ltd
Paycocke Road
Basildon
Essex SS14 3DR
Tel: 0268 27788

Kord Audio Products Ltd
7 The Green
Nettleham
near Lincoln LN2 2NR
Tel: 0522 750702

Lenson Heath Ltd
Unit 75
Wooburn Park Industrial Estate
Wooburn Green
Buckinghamshire HP10 0PF
Tel: 06285 25887

Luxor (UK) Ltd
87–9 Farnham Road
Slough
Berkshire SL1 4UL
Tel: 0753 36036

L & S Bear Electronics Ltd
Unit E
Yeo Lane
Colley Lane Industrial Estate
Bridgwater
Somerset TA6 5JJ
Tel: 0278 421719

Maspro
C. Itoh & Co., Ltd
London International Press Centre
76 Shoe Lane
London EC4A 3JB
Tel: 01 353 6090

Megasat Ltd
5 St Pancras Commercial Centre
Pratt Street
London NW1 0BY
Tel: 01 267 5222

Microsat Ltd
12 North Portway Close
Round Spinney
Northampton NR3 4RQ
Tel: 0604 493232

Micro-X Ltd
765–7 Harrow Road
London NW10 5NY
Tel: 01 968 6622

Multipoint Communications Ltd
Satellite House
Eastways Industrial Park
Witham
Essex CM8 3YQ
Tel: 0376 510881

NEC Business Systems (Europe) Ltd
35 Oval Road
London NW1 7EA
Tel: 01 267 7000

Network Services
Units 1 & 2
Newburn Bridge Industrial Estate
Hartlepool
Cleveland TS25 1UB
Tel: 0429 274239

Nissho Iwai (UK) Ltd
Bastion House
140 London Wall
London EC2Y 5JT
Tel: 01 628 6030

Orbitel Satellite Systems
Linnear Court
16–20 Cumberland Street South
Dublin 2
Republic of Ireland
Tel: 0001 714 677

Philips Consumer Electronics Ltd
City House
420–30 London Road
Croydon CR9 3QR
Tel: 01 689 2166

The Beginner's Guide to Satellite TV

Rediffusion Radio Systems Ltd
Unit 9
Mole Business Park
Randalls Road
Leatherhead
Surrey KT22 7BA
Tel: 0372 379620

Salora (UK) Ltd
Techno Trading Estate
Swindon
Wiltshire SN2 6EZ
Tel: 0793 644223

Satellite Technology Systems Ltd
Satellite House
Blackswarth Road
Bristol BS5 8AU
Tel: 0272 554535

Sat-Tel
Space Communications Ltd
9 Edgemead Close
Round Spinney
Northampton NN3 4RG
Tel: 0604 499433

Satvrn
Satellite TV Antenna Systems Ltd
10 Market Square
Staines
Middlesex TW18 4RH
Tel: 0784 65666

Appendices

Skyscan Ltd
Unit 2
Priors Way
Maidenhead
Berkshire SL6 2HP
Tel: 0628 783031

Telsat Communications Ltd
Marinsped House
98–102 Ley Street
Ilford
Essex IG1 4BX
Tel: 01 514 0768

Trac Satellite Systems
18 High Street
Stokesley
Middlesbrough
Cleveland TS9 5DQ
Tel: 0642 468145

Vusat Ltd
Intex Building 2
Wade Road
Basingstoke
Hampshire RG24 0NE
Tel: 0256 473232

The Beginner's Guide to Satellite TV

Appendix 3: Programme providers and management organizations

Addresses

The Arts Channel
P.O. Box 7
Ebbw Vale
Gwent
South Wales NP3 5YP
Tel: 0495 306965

Business Television Network (BTN)
Paul Winner Consultants
140 Sloane Street
London SWIX 4AY
Tel: 01 730 8525

Cable News Network (CNN)
Turner Broadcasting International
4th Floor
66–7 Newman Street
London WIP 3LA
Tel: 01 631 5278

The Children's Channel
44–6 Whitfield Street
London WIP 5RF
Tel: 01 580 6611

Europa Television
P.O. Box 1800
1200 Hilversum
The Netherlands
Tel: 010 31 35 7780 61

Appendices

Eutelstat
Tour Maine-Montparnasse
33 Avenue du Maine
75755 Paris
France
Tel: 010 1 538 4747

Filmnet
ATN Filmnet
Keizerssracht 319
1015 EE
Amsterdam
Holland
Tel: 010 31 20 557 7711

INTELSAT
490 L'Enfant Plaza SW
Washington DC 20024
USA
Tel: 010 1 202 488 2300

Lifestyle
The Quadrangle
180 Wardour Street
London W1V 4AE
Tel: 01 439 1177

Premiere
5 D'Arblay Street
London W1V 3FD
Tel: 01 434 0611

RAI-Uno
Viale Mazzini 14
00195 Rome 1
Tel: 010 39 6 38781

The Beginner's Guide to Satellite TV

RTL Plus
P.O. Box 2820
Luxembourg
Tel: 010 352 449 041

Sat-1
Heggle Strasse 61
D-6500 Mainzert
Anlage 2–40
West Germany
Tel: 010 40 637090

Satellite Programme Clearing House
The Quadrangle
180 Wardour Street
London WIV 4AE
Tel: 01 439 0075

Screen Sport
The Quadrangle
180 Wardour Street
London WIV 4AE
Tel: 01 439 1177

Sky Channel
Satellite Television plc
31/36 Foley Street
London WIP 7LB
Tel: 01 636 4077

Société Européenne des Satellites (SES)
63 Avenue de la Liberté
1931 Luxembourg
Tel: 010 352 496927

Appendices

Superchannel
19–21 Rathbone Place
London W1P 1DF
Tel: 01 636 7888

Teleclub
Fluelastrasse 7
Postfach CH8048
Zürich
Switzerland
Tel: 010 492 4433

TV5
Sattelimage
21 Rue Goujon
75008
Paris
France
Tel: 010 1 4299 4125

W. H. Smith & Sons Television Services
The Quadrangle
180 Wardour Street
London W1V 4AE
Tel: 01 439 1177

Technical Data

Times given below are BST (British Standard Time). Most channels that broadcast from the Continent operate on CET (Central European Time), which is one hour ahead of BST. 'Status' refers to the current situation with regard to encryption or scrambling, and whether or not it is a subscription channel (sub.). STV dealers will usually advise on how and where payments are to be made. A number of other TV channels (or, more correctly, 'links' or 'feeds') used by various TV companies can be received from other satellites. However, advance notice of this material is not normally available.

The Arts Channel

Satellite: Intelsat V-FII
Frequency: 11.175 gigahertz
Polarity: horizontal
Times: 06.00 to 09.00
Language: English
Status: clear (sub.)

Business Television Network (BTN)

Satellite: ECS-F-2
Frequency: Transponder 2
Polarity: horizontal
Times: 23.30 to 00.30
Language: English
Status: clear

Cable News Network (CNN)

Satellite: Intelsat V-FII
Frequency: 11.155 gigahertz
Polarity: vertical
Times: 24 hours
Language: English
Status: clear

The Children's Channel

Satellite: Intelsat V-FII
Frequency: 11.015 gigahertz
Polarity: horizontal
Times: 07.00 to 15.00
Language: English
Status: clear (sub.)

Europa Television

Satellite: ECS-FI
Frequency: 11.170 gigahertz
Polarity: horizontal
Times: 17.30 to 23.30
Language: English, Dutch, Portuguese
Status: clear

Filmnet

Satellite: ECS-FI
Frequency: 11.138 gigahertz
Polarity: vertical
Times: 24 hours
Language: English (Dutch subtitles)
Status: scrambled (Matsushita)

Lifestyle

Satellite: Intelsat V-FII
Frequency: 11.135 gigahertz
Polarity: horizontal
Times: 09.00 to 13.00
Language: English
Status: clear (sub.)

Premiere

Satellite: Intelsat V-FII
Frequency: 11.015 gigahertz
Polarity: horizontal
Times: 15.00 to 03.00
Language: English (stereo)
Status: clear (sub.)

RAI-Uno

Satellite: ECS-F1
Frequency: 11.005 gigahertz
Polarity: horizontal
Times: 12.00 to 24.00
Language: Italian
Status: clear

RTL Plus

Satellite: ECS-F1
Frequency: 11.085 gigahertz
Polarity: vertical
Times: 15.00 to 19.00
Language: German
Status: clear

Sat-1

Satellite: ECS-F1
Frequency: 11.507 gigahertz
Polarity: vertical
Times: 14.00 to 24.00
Language: German (plus two radio channels)
Status: clear

Screen Sport

Satellite: Intelsat V-F11
Frequency: 11.135 gigahertz
Polarity: horizontal
Times: 16.00 to 24.00
Language: English
Status: clear (sub.)

Appendices

Sky Channel

Satellite: ECS-FI
Frequency: 11.650 gigahertz
Polarity: horizontal
Times: 07.00 to 24.00
Language: English
Status: scrambled (Oak/Orion)

Superchannel

Satellite: ECS-FI
Frequency: 11.674
Polarity: vertical
Times: 24 hours
Language: English
Status: clear (sub.)

Teleclub

Satellite: ECS-FI
Frequency: 10.986 gigahertz
Polarity: vertical
Times: 15.00 to 01.00
Language: German
Status: clear

TV5

Satellite: ECS-FI
Frequency: 11.470 gigahertz
Polarity: horizontal
Times: 16.00 to 24.00
Language: French
Status: clear (monochrome picture)

Glossary

This section contains terms that readers are likely to encounter in STV literature.

AFC Automatic frequency control. An electronic circuit within a tuner/receiver that 'locks' on to the frequency of an incoming broadcast signal to ensure optimum reception.

AGC Automatic gain control. In effect, an automatic volume control circuit that adjusts the amplification (or gain) in a receiver system to ensure that the output signal remains constant irrespective of variations in the incoming signals.

analogue Literally, a descriptive term to indicate that something has a direct physical similarity to the thing it represents or encodes – like the grooves in a gramophone record, which correspond to the actual pattern of sonic impulses recorded. In electronic terms it is roughly the opposite of 'digital', i.e. it describes anything that has a continuously variable state or condition, as opposed to one chopped up into a succession of numerical 'bits', or values. See also *digital*.

antenna A metallic device connected to a receiver that is designed to respond to specific bands of electromagnetic radio-frequency signals. The operating frequencies and function determine the form, which can be anything from a simple length of wire to a complex parabolically shaped dish.

apogee The point in a satellite's (or any other object's or vehicle's) orbital trajectory when it is at its furthest point from the Earth.

Arabsat A system of communications and broadcast satellites first launched in 1984 by the Arab League Regional Communications Satellites System.

Ariane Non-reusable launch vehicle system operated by the European Space Agency.

attenuation The process of reducing the strength of a signal. This can happen deliberately, using a device known as an attenuator, or naturally, e.g. as a radio signal passes through the Earth's atmosphere or through a long cable or wire.

azimuth angle An angle of horizontal rotation (normally measured with respect to magnetic north) that will describe an arc between the horizon and the sky (usually passing through the point at which a satellite is located in its geostationary orbit).

baseband The video signal in its most basic form – essentially the 'raw' video signal before it is processed prior to being fed to a television receiver. A baseband video output socket is fitted to most STV demodulators; this is intended to allow connection with some types of signal decoders, or unscramblers, which require an unadulterated signal to work correctly. Many decoders also have sockets marked 'video output'; this is normally a standard 1-volt (peak-to-peak) processed signal, suitable for feeding directly into TV monitors or VCRs.

bird American nickname for a satellite.

buttonhook feed A type of dish in which the LNB is mounted on a single mounting pole fixed to the centre of the dish. It is known as a 'buttonhook' feed because of the hooklike bends in the mounting point, which ensure that the LNB is sited at the dish's focal point.

carrier A radio signal used to 'carry' video, audio or data transmissions by a process known as modulation, whereby the desired information is used to vary electronically either the carrier's amplitude (AM or amplitude modulation) or its frequency (FM or frequency modulation). Normal terrestrial TV broadcasts use a combination of AM and FM transmissions; satellite TV signals are almost entirely FM.

carrier frequency The frequency of the carrier signal, measured in Hertz (formerly known as cycles per second). Ordinary UHF TV signals in the UK have carrier frequencies of 600 to 800 megahertz (800,000,000 hertz). US satellite broadcasts are typically on the 4 gigahertz (4,000,000,000 hertz) band, while most European satellites operate between 11 and 12 gigahertz.

cassegrain antenna A parabolic dish-type antenna using a small sub-reflector mounted at its focal point. Energy from the sub-antenna is reflected back to a pick-up device (LNC) mounted at the apex of the dish.

C-band The 4 to 6 gigahertz band used on some US and international communications satellites.

channel A specific frequency band occupied by one broadcast signal.

circular polarization A corkscrewlike signal pattern broadcast from a satellite's antenna. See also *polarization*, horizontal and vertical.

Clarke Belt A nickname for the orbital path, first suggested by Arthur C. Clarke in 1945, 36,000 kilometres above the Earth's surface, where geosynchronous satellites are placed. Satellites in

Glossary

this orbit, travelling at nearly 62,000 mph to match the Earth's rotation, appear to remain stationary above the planet's surface.

CNR Carrier-to-noise ratio: a measurement of the ratio of a received satellite signal to electromagnetic noise, quoted in decibels.

coaxial cable A type of connecting cable designed to carry high-frequency signals. Coaxial leads have a single central conductor suspended inside a woven outer conductor. This arrangement prevents both signal loss and interference from other, external radio-frequency signals.

Comsat Communications Satellite Corporation: the organization responsible for the launching and operation of satellites for the Intelsat group of countries. Comsat also owns and operates a number of Comstar satellites over the US.

DBS Direct broadcasting by satellite: a new generation of high-power satellites that will ultimately replace terrestrial (land-based) transmission systems. DBS transmissions will be receivable on small (typically less than a metre in diameter) dish antennas. Current satellite transmissions are low to medium power and can be received only on larger dishes (typically 1.2 to 1.8 metres).

decibel A mathematical term used to express ratios logarithmically between two quantities.

declination The offset angle of a dish antenna in relation to its own horizontal plane. A measurement used to align polar mounts where the antenna has to follow an arc across the sky.

demodulator Part of a satellite receiver designed to extract video and audio information from the incoming signal.

digital A technique of storing, transferring or retrieving information in mathematically encoded form. The signals used normally have just two distinct states, and data is sent in a stream of pulses, largely immune to interference or corruption, which can be readily processed by computers and similar digitally based equipment. See also *analogue*.

down converter A device or circuit used to convert high-frequency signals to lower, more easily manageable frequencies.

downlink The transmission path from an orbiting satellite to a receiving dish.

earth station A ground-based transmitter or receiving system designed to pick up or transmit signals from or to an orbiting satellite.

ECS/Eutelsat European Telecommunications Satellite System: a series of satellites in geostationary orbit over Europe, carrying a mixture of TV and communications signals.

EIRP Effective Isotropic Radiated Power: a measurement of a satellite's transmission power, calculated by analysing the strength of the signal received on Earth.

elaz mount An antenna mounting system designed to allow a dish to move through vertical (elevation) and horizontal (azimuth) planes.

elevation angle The angle or tilt in a dish antenna, measured in degrees in relation to the horizon (which is designated zero degrees), e.g. an antenna pointed directly overhead would have an elevation angle of 90 degrees.

encryption A technique used to disseminate electronically and restructure, or encode, a television signal (in the case of STV) prior to its being transmitted via a satellite link. A specialized decoder has to be fitted to an STV tuner or a TV receiver in order to reprocess the signal into a form suitable for viewing. Encryption is likely to be used as a means of collecting revenue from viewers. Some advanced types of decoders will operate on a pay-per-view basis, requiring the viewer to insert a pre-payment magnetic card (similar to a Phonecard) into a slot in the unit before it will work. See also *scrambling*.

feedhorn An antenna component used to collect the signal reflected from the surface of the dish and feed it into the LNC.

footprint The terrestrial area over which a satellite transmission can be received (normally shown on a map by contourlike lines joining points of equal signal strength).

gain A measure of the increase in level or strength of a signal as it passes from one element in a system to another, normally expressed as a ratio and measured in decibels.

GasFet Gallium arsenide field effect transistor: the key component inside the microwave head.

Ghorizont A series of Russian satellites, normally used as part of a relay system to rebroadcast signals. Transmissions from Ghorizont 2, located at 14 degrees west, can be received over most of Europe.

gigahertz 1,000,000,000 hertz, or cycles, per second: a measure of frequency. Radio frequency signals above 1 gigahertz are normally referred to as 'microwaves' and begin to exhibit some of the characteristics of visible light.

global beam Satellite transmission beam designed to cover as much of the Earth's surface as possible.

half transponder A technique used to transmit two STV signals through a single transponder. Half transponder signals can be weaker and noiser than full transponder signals.

high-power satellite A satellite operating with transmitter powers of 100 watts or above.

INTELSAT International Telecommunications Organization: owns and operates the global satellite communications system used to carry television and telephone transmissions to all parts of the world. The Intelsat organization is based in Washington DC.

KU-band Band of frequencies in the range 10.7 to 12.75 gigahertz, used for most European satellite transmissions.

low-power satellite A satellite operating with transmitter power levels below 30 watts.

LNA Low-noise amplifier. A device attached to the feedhorn of an antenna, designed to amplify the extremely weak signals being received by the dish.

LNB/LNC Low-noise block converter/low-noise converter: a device attached to the feedhorn of an antenna that picks up satellite signals and converts them to a lower, more easily manageable frequency.

MAC Multiplexed analogue component: a high-quality transmission standard devised specifically for DBS satellite broadcasting and high-definition TV systems. Variations include B-MAC (developed by the BBC), C-MAC (developed by the IBA), D-MAC (high-definition system) and D2-MAC.

medium-power satellite A satellite operating with transmitter power levels of 30 to 100 watts.

microwave An electronic radio frequency signal or carrier above 1 gigahertz.

Glossary

Newtonian feed A type of indirect-feed dish with a tubular waveguide that is mounted on the LNB and pointing at an inverted conical reflector mounted at the focal point.

noise temperature A measure of the noise added to the received signal during the initial stages of processing. Noise temperature is normally expressed in degrees Kelvin, a scale in which zero degrees corresponds to 'absolute' zero (-459 °F).

NTSC National Television Standards Committee: TV transmission standard used in the US and much of the Far East.

offset feed antenna Antenna design, usually elliptical (sometimes square), where the LNB is outside of the incoming signal path.

orthogonal mode transducer A microwave waveguide component that separates or combines signals of opposing polarity.

PAL Phase Alternate Line: TV transmission standard used in the UK, Europe and Australia.

parabolic antenna The most common type of dish antenna configuration. The curved, parabolic shape acts like a concave mirror and focuses the extremely weak microwave signal on a single point where the feedhorn and LNC are located.

perigee The point in an orbital trajectory that is closest to the Earth's surface.

petalized A method of construction used in some antennae where the dish is built up from a number of identically shaped 'petals' bolted together.

polarization A transmission technique used to increase a satellite's signal capacity. Polarization allows a single transmitter element, or transponder, to beam two signals simultaneously on the same frequency. One of the two main methods involves horizontally and vertically polarized signals sharing the same transponder; the other variation is to use circular polarization, in which signals are given right-hand and left-hand orientation. In order to receive a polarized signal the LNCs mounted on the dish must be similarly polarized.

polar mount Also equatorial mount. A mounting system that allows a dish to track or scan the line of geosynchronous satellites.

rain outage Drop in STV signal level and rise in noise levels during heavy rain storms.

Satcom A series of US satellites that give some degree of coverage to Europe.

S-band Signals transmitted on a band of frequencies between 2.5 and 4 gigahertz.

scrambling An electronic process used to deliberately corrupt a television signal (in the case of STV), making it completely unwatchable on a normal, unmodified television receiver. Unlike encryption, which totally reconfigures the information contained within the signal, scrambling maintains the basic structure of the signal. A decoder, built into the STV demodulator or TV receiver, is required to 'unscramble' the signal, turning it into a form suitable for viewing. See also *encryption*.

SECAM Séquentielle Couleur à Mémoire: TV transmission standard used in France, the USSR and Cuba.

SES Société Européenne des Satellites: Luxembourg-based consortium backing the sixteen-channel, medium-power satellite, Astra.

signal-to-noise ratio (S/N) The measurement of the power or strength of a signal, expressed as a ratio between the signal itself and the level or strength of the noise within it. S/N ratio is normally rated in decibels: a high value implies a better, clearer picture.

SMATV Satellite master antenna television: a term used to describe STV equipment that acts as the basis for a cable TV system.

Glossary

sparklies An apt description for a form of signal interference that takes the form of bright, sparkling dots or flashes on the TV picture.

spot beam Carefully controlled transmission beam from a satellite, intended to cover only a relatively small area of the Earth's surface. (Opposite 'Global beam'.)

SWR Standing wave ratio: a measurement of an antenna system's tuning efficiency.

threshold extension An electronic technique used in satellite receivers to improve the CNR.

transponder Also repeater. The components in a satellite that are responsible for receiving, processing and retransmitting a signal up from and back down to the Earth.

TVRO Television receive-only: a basic satellite broadcast receiving system. The term is now commonly used to describe domestic installations.

uplink The transmission path from an earth station up to a satellite.

wind loading A measurement of the pressure imparted on a satellite dish by the force of wind. A well-designed installation should be able to withstand wind speeds of up to 50 mph without any noticeable loss of picture quality.

FOR THE BEST IN PAPERBACKS, LOOK FOR THE 🐧

In every corner of the world, on every subject under the sun, Penguins represent quality and variety – the very best in publishing today.

For complete information about books available from Penguin and how to order them, write to us at the appropriate address below. Please note that for copyright reasons the selection of books varies from country to country.

In the United Kingdom: For a complete list of books available from Penguin in the U.K., please write to *Dept EP, Penguin Books Ltd, Harmondsworth, Middlesex, UB7 0DA*

In the United States: For a complete list of books available from Penguin in the U.S., please write to *Dept BA, Viking Penguin, 299 Murray Hill Parkway, East Rutherford, New Jersey 07073*

In Canada: For a complete list of books available from Penguin in Canada, please write to *Penguin Books Canada Limited, 2801 John Street, Markham, Ontario L3R 1B4*

In Australia: For a complete list of books available from Penguin in Australia, please write to the *Marketing Department, Penguin Books Australia Ltd, P.O. Box 257, Ringwood, Victoria 3134*

In New Zealand: For a complete list of books available from Penguin in New Zealand, please write to the *Marketing Department, Penguin Books (N.Z.) Ltd, Private Bag, Takapuna, Auckland 9*

In India: For a complete list of books available from Penguin in India, please write to *Penguin Overseas Ltd, 706 Eros Apartments, 56 Nehru Place, New Delhi 110019*

FOR THE BEST IN PAPERBACKS, LOOK FOR THE 🐧

PENGUIN REFERENCE BOOKS

The Penguin English Dictionary

Over 1,000 pages long and with over 68,000 definitions, this cheap, compact and totally up-to-date book is ideal for today's needs. It includes many technical and colloquial terms, guides to pronunciation and common abbreviations.

The Penguin Reference Dictionary

The ideal comprehensive guide to written and spoken English the world over, with detailed etymologies and a wide selection of colloquial and idiomatic usage. There are over 100,000 entries and thousands of examples of how words are actually used – all clear, precise and up-to-date.

The Penguin English Thesaurus

This unique volume will increase anyone's command of the English language and build up your word power. Fully cross-referenced, it includes synonyms of every kind (formal or colloquial, idiomatic and figurative) for almost 900 headings. It is a must for writers and utterly fascinating for any English speaker.

The Penguin Dictionary of Quotations

A treasure-trove of over 12,000 new gems and old favourites, from Aesop and Matthew Arnold to Xenophon and Zola.

FOR THE BEST IN PAPERBACKS, LOOK FOR THE 🐧

PENGUIN REFERENCE BOOKS

The Penguin Guide to the Law

This acclaimed reference book is designed for everyday use, and forms the most comprehensive handbook ever published on the law as it affects the individual.

The Penguin Medical Encyclopedia

Covers the body and mind in sickness and in health, including drugs, surgery, history, institutions, medical vocabulary and many other aspects. 'Highly commendable' – *Journal of the Institute of Health Education*

The Penguin French Dictionary

This invaluable French-English, English-French dictionary includes both the literary and dated vocabulary needed by students, and the up-to-date slang and specialized vocabulary (scientific, legal, sporting, etc) needed in everyday life. As a passport to the French language, it is second to none.

A Dictionary of Literary Terms

Defines over 2,000 literary terms (including lesser known, foreign language and technical terms) explained with illustrations from literature past and present.

The Penguin Map of Europe

Covers all land eastwards to the Urals, southwards to North Africa and up to Syria, Iraq and Iran. Scale – 1:5,500,000, 4-colour artwork. Features main roads, railways, oil and gas pipelines, plus extra information including national flags, currencies and populations.

The Penguin Dictionary of Troublesome Words

A witty, straightforward guide to the pitfalls and hotly disputed issues in standard written English, illustrated with examples and including a glossary of grammatical terms and an appendix on punctuation.